You Can Visit,
but You Can't Live There

Keys to Living Free from Fear, Anxiety, and Guilt

Amy L. Travis

ISBN 978-1-7335626-9-0

Cover photo and design courtesy of Susan McConville-Harrer

Edited by Christy Callahan

Photograph on back cover by Jason Swanson

Printed in the United States of America

Published by SMH Illustration & Design
123 S Third ST, Youngwood, PA 15697
www.smhillustration.com

fusion.group.pgh@gmail.com
https://www.fusionleadership.site/

TABLE OF CONTENTS

DEDICATION

To my father, Tom Geier,
who taught me the value of living until you die

What Is Resiliency?

Picture this scenario: two young men try out for the high school football team, and both players are cut. Player A and player B trained equally hard all summer with the team, and they had the expectation that they would be on the field come Friday night. Player A and player B are both crushed because of being cut from the squad. They feel humiliated, left out, and angry. They may trash-talk the coaches to their teammates as they leave the locker room. Once home, they slam the bedroom door and refuse to come down for dinner that night.

Here's where the difference becomes evident: Player A may still be angry and frustrated, but he goes to the game the following Friday. He has to find a new group of friends since most of his friends are on the field. He may even volunteer to keep statistics in order to stay involved and increase his chances of making the team next year. Player B, however, spends that Friday night locked in his room. He posts angry comments on social media and blames the coaches, players, or other kids' parents. He may even make threats. This behavior goes on for weeks and even months.

Player B eventually gives up football all together and refuses to join any other teams or clubs.

Why is it that, in this era of tremendous prosperity, so many individuals struggle with anxiety-related issues? An estimated one in three Americans will struggle with anxiety at some point in their lives, with hardest hit demographic being women ages eighteen to twenty-nine.[1] Our stress related to work, school, and relationships seems to be increasing exponentially. This is a phenomenon for which there is no good explanation.

But there's good news.

If there's one characteristic that could guarantee that we would excel in this life, it would be RESILIENCE. *Resiliency* is the ability to become strong, healthy, or successful again after something bad happens. This trait is often credited with guarding against depression and anxiety and can enable one to overcome trauma and grief even in extreme circumstances. This ability is not limited by one's age, race, or social status.

Building resilience isn't expensive or complex and doesn't require great resources or physical strength. In fact, it is free and available to all of us! It starts by recognizing that we're the captain of our own ship. We can't control the wind, but we can always adjust the sails.[2]

One point that I often stressed to my players during my ten years coaching high school and college soccer was the need to "play the ball, and not let the ball play you." It was important to know what play you would make before the ball even came near your zone. Do you need to get into position to be able to receive the ball? Do you have an open player down field? Is a defender quickly approaching from behind? Or, do you have time to control the ball and allow your team to push forward? Simply reacting to the ball is not only ineffective—it can be dangerous. Not being prepared to receive the ball could leave a player in a vulnerable position. Skilled, competent players are those who can anticipate the play and act decisively when the opportunity comes.

Your ability to be resilient and control the narrative in your life works in a similar way. The thoughts you think and choices you make before you hit rough waters will determine the course you ultimately chart for yourself. *You Can Visit, but You Can't Live* There is a how-to guide providing anecdotal responses to common problems that prevent us from living the happy, meaningful lives for which God created us…free from fear, anxiety, and guilt. Below is a summary of the topics we will discuss:

- *The Key to Unlocking Your Potential*
  History has been made throughout the ages when average people facing insurmountable circumstances rejected the naysayers and conventional wisdom that said that they did not have a choice. This chapter provides examples of these brave individuals and how we can forge our own path.

- *The Key to Not Losing Your Mind*
  Schedule overload may seem like a simple problem of too little time, but the Bible makes it clear that the battle starts in our minds. Our calendars don't clutter themselves. The root of this problem is what things we deem to be urgent or important. This chapter will explore how to focus on what's truly important.

- *The Key to Contentment*
  As human beings, we are terrible at predicting what will make us happy. In fact, we often find that getting what we want often makes us unhappy. Sometimes the unfortunate situations that we would never choose—the ones that we fear the most—that can be the pathway to true contentment.

- *The Key to Becoming Resilient*
  Why is it that two people can experience the same traumatic event, but have two very different responses? Resiliency is defined as the ability to become strong and healthy again after something bad happens. We will explore how we can bounce back, even from tragedy and loss.

- *The Key to Raising Resilient Children*
  Because our children live in this age of prosperity, they will never have to overcome the insurmountable odds that our grandparents and great-grandparents did when immigrating to this country and living through the Great Depression. That's the good news. The bad news is, I'm not sure that they could. We will explore how we can build the same resiliency in our children without them having to experience the hardships of previous generations.

- *The Key to Eliminating Unproductive Guilt*
  For many, feelings of guilt are so common that we wear them around as we would a purse, belt, or scarf. We are so accustomed to feeling guilty that we carry around this excess baggage like it's our job. We will address how we can make guilt productive, not destructive, in our lives.

- *The Key to Overcoming Failure*
  Telling ourselves that failure isn't an option is not only unproductive but can create a tremendous amount of anxiety. We will discuss how throughout history, some of the most ground-breaking successes came on the heels of epic failures…and why failure can be an important part of our success story.

- *The Key to Overcoming Irrational Fear*
  Fear, like guilt and other emotions, serves a purpose
  in the human experience. Fear should cause us to be
  alert. Rational fear keeps us from doing anything stupid,
  but irrational fear prevents us from doing anything
  useful. We will discuss how to conduct a risk assessment
  in order to determine the difference.

- *The Key to Being Kind, Not Just Acting It*
  Like everything else in our culture, kindness has
  become performance based. The trouble is, performing
  acts of kindness is easy, even when our motives aren't
  pure. We will explore how making kindness part of our
  character—not just part of our behavior—can lead to
  deep, meaningful relationships.

- *The Key to Being Free*
  Being free means thinking for yourself and not hiding
  behind the crowd. The crowd does not have your best
  interest in mind and can never truly represent you.
  Living Free means pursuing the truth—God's truth.

Know this: it's ok to be frustrated, disappointed, and even angry. It's ok to feel ripped off, because sometimes—let's face it—we are. It's ok to feel hurt, betrayed, or backstabbed. We don't deserve to be treated that way. It's ok to feel sad, devastated, and alone after experiencing a gut-wrenching loss. But here's the thing…
You can visit, but you can't live there.

Be an Independent Contractor

The Key to Unlocking Your Potential

I grew up as the oldest of three kids with two younger brothers. The women were definitely outnumbered. As is the case in many households my father was an avid sports fan and my brothers' baseball and soccer practices completely dominated the day-to-day schedule. Because my parents insisted on eating dinner together as a family, this often didn't happen until 9 p.m. at night in the summer. I remember from a very early age that the talk at the dinner table always revolved around sports.

I was eleven years old when I made the conscious decision that I either needed to be involved in sports, or I was going to be left behind. So one day at dinner I announced that I was signing up for junior high cross country. I had never run a mile in my life up to that point, but I so badly wanted to be part of a team.

I still remember my dad's response. He laughed involuntary and said, "You'll never finish the season."

Well, it was game on. I had to prove him wrong

because, even then, I had a stubborn streak. This was back in the 1980s when there was just one junior high team, and I happened to be the only girl. Not only was I competing against seventh-, eighth-, and ninth-grade boys, but I was incredibly slow, even for a girl. I took finishing last to a whole new level—"packing up the truck and turning off the lights" last place. One time I even got lost in the woods because I was so far behind the pack. (This was, to my dismay, my father's favorite story to tell every family dinner for the next 30 years.) It was one of the most miserable two months of my life.

But of course, I finished the season. Not only was my dad at every meet, but he took me out on a date after the season to celebrate that I made it through.

Dad was a very wise man who was widely respected by many. He also had a stubborn streak a mile wide. He understood that discipline was a rare virtue and the key to achieving success. He always encouraged me to think for myself and then follow through with my decisions. Even though he was often annoyed by my stubbornness, he was proud of the fact that the apple didn't fall far from the proverbial tree. He used to introduce me to his friends as his "independent contractor." That was his way of saying, *Look out! Don't get in her way.*

It wasn't until I got older that I recognized there was actually such a thing as an independent contractor. Dad was an accountant, so independent contractor (IC) was a tax filing status. It simply meant that you didn't work for another organization, and as a result, you were responsible for your own wages, benefits, and taxes.

The fact of the matter is that we're all independent contractors. No, I'm not talking about your status for filing taxes with the IRS. I'm talking about the fact that we are all responsible for own lives and our own business. As adults we often take our identity from our work or family, but at the end of the day we can't blame our action (or inaction) on our boss, our spouse, our children, or our parents. "He made me do it," doesn't fly when we're older than ten years old. There is no fall guy to take the blame or credit for our choices. God has given us everything we need to lead successful, full lives on this earth.³ There are no excuses and no one to blame when we don't make it happen. We are independent contractors.

With all of the opportunity presented, why do so many of us feel that we are not in control of our own destiny? Why is it that, in the most prosperous time, in arguably the greatest country in the world, we are seeing a higher prevalence of anxiety disorders than any other period in history? Researchers estimate that 19.1 percent of adults in the United States suffered with anxiety disorders in 2017. Females between the ages of eighteen to twenty-nine report the highest rate of occurrence at 23.4 percent.⁴ It would appear that in "the Land of the Free," more of us are living in a self-imposed captivity than at any time in history. The principles defined in *You can Visit, but You Can't Live There* are designed to release us so that we can pursue the life and purpose for which God created us—free from the bondage of fear, anxiety, and guilt.

Own Everything in Your Life

If we are going to Live Free, we have to recognize that we have a position of responsibility in our own lives. For everything that happens, we are responsible: the good, the bad, and the ugly. As healthy, productive adults, God has given us everything we need to be the captains of our own ships.

It sounds easy enough, but it's not.

The urge to shirk personal responsibility doesn't automatically go away when we turn eighteen and become an adult. To further complicate things, there are others who would gladly exert control in our lives: a parent, a spouse, or close friend. Sometimes this is an innocent mistake by a well-meaning friend or relative. Other times, this can be a part of a more devious plan to control and manipulate us.

Steven Covey, author of *Seven Habits of Highly Effective People*, said, "If we don't make a conscience decision on who we want to be and what we will do, then someone else will make those choices for us."[5] We all know of people in our lives who would gladly control our lives and futures if we allowed them.

As much as I hate to admit it, I was in my early forties and still wondering what I wanted to be when I grew up. *We need to decide who we want to be...seriously?*

It takes a lot of work to be an independent contractor. I think that's why so many us abdicate this responsibility to our parents, spouse, or friend. I can tell you from experience that parents love to make decisions for their kids: what career to pursue, who to marry, where to live. It's actually a standing joke in my family that my marriage to Perry was arranged by my parents! (That's not exactly how it went, but isn't too far off either. That's a story for later.) The bottom line is, if we don't decide for ourselves, there are plenty of people standing in line to make those decisions for us.

Sometimes, the problem isn't that we don't make decisions; it's that we make the wrong ones. Our poor choices can dictate our direction in life by limiting our options. Accumulating debt in early adulthood, for example, can be a spurious factor in determining our path forward. It's an open secret that higher college debt is a contributing factor to why so many millennials are opting to live at home.

In fact, there are several areas that we must monitor continually if we are going to take control and remain in control of our own lives:

1. Our physical health – Controlling our weight and lifestyle choices is critical to Living Free.

2. Our financial independence – Limiting or eliminating our debt to other people and institutions will support our freedom.

3. Our relationships – Choosing healthy relationships and avoiding toxic ones will limit unnecessary emotional baggage.

4. Our emotions – Learning how to keep our emotions balanced and healthy will allow us to pursue our life goals.

These areas are much more interdependent that we may even realize. Poor relationship and money trouble will rot our health quicker than mostly anything else. Medical expenses relating to poor health habits will tax our finances and personal relationships. Broken relationships could potentially endanger our health and bankrupt us financially. Failing to keep our emotions in check could jeopardize our personal and professional relationships. And so, the cycle continues.

We Always Have a Choice

Sometimes, our captivity to fear and anxiety is the result of feeling that we are trapped and that we aren't in control. It's important to recognize that we always have a choice. Always. It may not be easy, popular, or without consequences, but the decision is still ours.

There's a classic scene in one of the very first shows of the TV series Madame Secretary. Elizabeth McCord was just appointed as secretary of state. She was an unlikely candidate, and this created some tension between her and her boss, Russell Jackson, the president's chief of staff. Mr. Jackson hires a stylist for her without her knowledge (apparently, he didn't like her look). The stylist shows up at McCord's office and announces that she needs to meet with the secretary ASAP.

When Secretary McCord makes it clear that the idea doesn't sit well with her, the woman replies, "Ma'am, I was sent by Russel Jackson's office. It appears that you don't have a choice."

Wait for it…

Secretary McCord stands up straight, looks the woman in the eye and declares boldly that *she has never been in a situation where she doesn't have a choice.*

And neither have you.

Even when it appears that we are out of options, we always have a choice. History has been made throughout the ages when average people facing insurmountable circumstances rejected the naysayers and conventional wisdom that said that they did not have a choice.

- Oprah Winfrey, the first black multi-billionaire in North America, didn't appear to have a choice growing up in abject poverty in rural Mississippi to a teenage single mother…but she did.

- The USA Olympic Hockey team, comprised of mostly amateur players who defeated the Soviet Union in the 1980 medal round, didn't appear to have a choice when up against the superior USSR, who had won five of the six previous Winter Olympic Games…but they did.

- J. K. Rowling, author of the best-selling series on record in modern history, Harry Potter, didn't appear to have a choice as a struggling single mother on government subsidies…but she did.

- Winston Churchill, the politician and army officer credited with saving Europe from the stronghold of fascism, didn't appear to have a choice when England and surrounding countries were threatened by the Nazi regime…but he did.

- Jack Johnson, the first African American heavyweight champion of the world, was too poor to hire a coach, so he deliberately prolonged his fights so that he could learn more in the ring.[6] He didn't appear to have a choice as a poor black man born to former slaves…but he did.

What If It's Not My Fault?

I do want to stop for a minute and acknowledge that there are times when we suffer the consequences of other people's choices at no fault of our own. Every day innocent children are victimized by evil, self-serving adults. Entire populations have been denied basic human rights in places like Cuba, North Korea, and Venezuela. Even as citizens of a free country, there are still situations that are outside of our control. Some of you may have been in a relationship where you were faithful, but your spouse was not, for example.

Even if you've been victimized, you don't have to be a victim. You don't have to allow misfortune or tragedy to define you. Although it is not an easy process to prevent this from happening, it is certainly a battle worth fighting. Yielding to these feelings of helplessness and hopelessness give someone else control in your life. When you hang on to bitterness and resentment, it's like letting someone live rent-free in your head.[7]

Throughout this book we will discuss ways to pro-actively (or reactively, when necessary) process the emotions of fear, anxiety, guilt so that they do not control or define us as individuals.

The Wrap-Up

You are an independent contractor. No other human being owns you or should be allowed to control you. God has given you everything you need to live a productive life, free from the bondage of fear, anxiety, and guilt. This starts with recognizing that we always have a choice, regardless of how dire the situation appears, and how we choose to respond will determine what history writes about us.

"No" Your Limits

The Key to Not Losing Your Mind

One of the greatest experiences of my life came when I had the opportunity to speak at a leadership conference in Santa Clara, Cuba in February of 2015. The landscape was beautiful and the people we met were amazing, which reminded me of a Norman Rockwell painting from the 1960s, when life was much simpler.

I saw many things there that I would expect in a third-world country under Communist control, but a couple things caught me off guard. One was how sophisticated the infrastructure of the country was when its residents were so poor. The typical Cuban makes the equivalent of US$30 a month, regardless of their profession. Yes, their doctors are highly educated and skilled professionals making US$30 a month. And yet, they had beautifully paved roads and sound structures to bridge waterways, even though the vast majority of citizens will never be able to afford a car in their lifetime.

The roads leading into the cities even had the painted yellow lines. We all know that you should never cross the solid yellow line because you would be heading into oncoming traffic. Somehow that minor detail had escaped them. If you have ever ridden in a car or bus in a developing country, you know exactly what I'm talking about.

As the missionary was driving us back to the camp one day, I remember sitting at a T-shaped intersection, waiting to turn left. There were no traffic lights or stop signs to assist you. To further complicate matters, there were three "lanes" wide in each direction (on a two-lane road) of cars, trucks, bikes, motorized scooters, horse-and-buggy travelers, and pedestrians traveling at *all different* speeds. I thought I could have panic attack as I watched this scene. If I was driving that day, I think we may still be sitting there waiting to turn left.

It occurred to me recently that our lives can start to look an awful lot like this sensory-overloaded mishmash of objects flying in all different directions. We are so overwhelmed with obligations and commitments that we feel victimized by our schedules. Without traffic lights, stop signs, and other safety measures to direct traffic, our daily lives become marked by a level of chaos equal to trying to cross six lanes of traffic on a two-lane road in Cuba.

Schedule overload may seem like a simple problem of having too little time, but the battle starts in our minds. Our calendars don't clutter themselves. The root of this problem is what we deem to be important to us. As we talked about in chapter 2, we often don't take the initiative and allow someone else to set the priorities for us.

Battlespace awareness is a military term that the United States Department of Defense defines as the "knowledge and understanding of the operational area's environment, factors and conditions, to include the status of friendly and adversary forces, weather and terrain, that enables timely, relevant, comprehensive, and accurate assessments, in order to successfully complete the mission."[8]

Whether we realize it or not, our mind is our battlespace.[9] Our actions, attitudes, and motives originate here. Any project that we complete, event that we plan, goal that we reach, or structure that we build has to be created first in our minds. For every success there are a thousand other plans that are shot down in our brains (pun intended) before they can materialize.

The idea that there is an ongoing battle for control of our minds is a foreign concept to most Americans, but is spelled out very clearly in the Bible. It can freak people out when we start talking about strongholds, and taking our thoughts captive, but consider this: What is mental illness? Why do some individuals develop antisocial behaviors? What is the root of anxiety and depression? *It all starts in the mind.* If we are to Live Free from fear, anxiety, and guilt, we have to increase awareness of how to protect and defend our battlespace. Throughout this book we will explore both offensive and defensive practices. Let's look at a few.

Take a Defensive Position

I remember when MTV first came out in 1981, back when they still showed music videos. I used to watch it for hours and hours at a time. One time, when my father was passing through the living room, he stopped and said, "Amy, doesn't watching that junk all day long affect your mind?" I assured him that it did not and that I could handle it. After all, what thirteen-year-old couldn't? I miss the days when I was that smart.

We tend to laugh at our grandparents and our older relatives who don't have smartphones and think that Instagram is a new type of Polaroid camera. I've stopped laughing and realized that they are on to something. Certainly, there are things I love about social media—for example, the fact that I can connect with classmates from high school. It gives me a greater appreciation for who they are now and what they have become. But at the same time, nothing has caused me more anxiety than when I have engaged in discussions about religion or politics on social media platforms. I don't do that anymore.

My daughter informed me that mom-shaming is a thing too. Ugh. I recently talked to a young mom who said that she avoids social media like the plague because of how vulnerable to criticism it makes her feel. Raising children is hard enough without the added pressure of sensing that you don't measure up to other moms, even when it's not true. I'm glad Facebook wasn't around when my kids were little.

Research tells us that the average American checks their phone every twelve minutes (that comes out to eighty times a day)![10] The impulse to look at our phones is so intense that it has been likened to a drug addict's cravings. Recent studies are showing that the blue light from our phones is a culprit in the startling increase in insomnia cases, resulting in hospitalization.[11] And that too much screen time is linked to a reduction in brain power in children ages eight to eleven.[12] I can only image what that does to my older, more cluttered brain.

Go on the Offense

Preserving and renewing our minds, however, is more than just a matter of limiting our exposure to social media. It has to do with feeding ourselves the type of information that will build and renew, not tear down, our cerebral capacities.[13] One of the most impacting exercises that I have ever participated in is the memorization of scriptures in the Bible. Starting when I was in high school and continuing as a young mother who had a lot of time on her hands, I committed hundreds if not thousands of verses to memory.

The remarkable thing is that even though I often can't remember what I had for breakfast, I can recall scriptures that I memorized over thirty years ago. This discipline has served me well throughout the years when faced with situations that threatened to bring more than just a healthy dose of anxiety.

Hopefully you can tell from reading this that I have also invested hours upon hours of reading books and articles in a variety of different subjects. When I was coaching high school and college soccer, I read books on strategy and tactics by successful coaches. When my kids were younger, I read a lot of parenting articles. Because of my obsession with the TV series *JAG* in the 1990s, I read countless books by military leaders (and still do) and studied the World War II era. When I returned to the work force, I read hundreds of articles from business forums on social media. Not only will reading make you a better conversationalist, but lifelong learning has been connected with staving off dementia and other forms of cognitive decline as we age.[14]

It wouldn't be right to conclude this section without mentioning the impact of diet on our minds, not to mention our bodies. There is an undeniable connection between our mind, body, and soul.[15] Nutrition is not my area of expertise, but can tell you that too much sugar and fried food messes with both my hips and my head. The concept of Living Free includes freedom from self-imposed health conditions resulting from poor diet and too little exercise.

My mother is, without question, the most influential person in my life. She has an amazingly magnetic personality, as well as real grit. She started gearing up her life's activities at an age when most people begin to think about retirement. Growing up in the 1950s, she had greater family responsibilities and less opportunity to play sports in her youth as young women do today. As a result, she led a very sedentary lifestyle…until she met my father. Because he was relentless about the benefits of exercise, she took up jogging in her early thirties. She admits that when she started, she could only run from one mailbox to the next before she needed to stop. Nonetheless, she ran her first half marathon at the age of forty-seven.

Now, at the reverse of that age (seventy-four), she still works part-time, walks three days a week, and lifts weights (though not her favorite thing to do) in order to build bone density and look better in sleeveless tops. She speaks frequently at our FUSION leadership conferences and is making the physically taxing journey to Uganda, Africa with my daughter and me this fall. Because she recognized the value of caring for her body, soul, and spirit, she can enjoy great health and prosperity at this time in her life.

Establish Limits and Boundaries

It has been speculated that firstborn children, and especially daughters, are prone to be people pleasers. I think many of us can attest to this. People pleasers tend to put the needs and even the wants of others ahead of their own. Even though people pleasing gets a bad rap, it isn't all bad. If it wasn't for even-tempered, happy-go-lucky, agreeable individuals who can mediate even tense situations, the United States would probably be at war with Canada.

But the problem comes when we start to believe that we don't have a choice.

We can start to feel such a strong sense of obligation to family members, bosses, and long-time friends that we think we would be a bad person to say no. The truth of the matter is that saying yes out of a sense of obligation means that we are saying no to someone or something else—our spouse, our children, our own health. We forget that if we don't care for ourselves and those in our immediate realm of responsibility, we are useless to anyone else. There have been a lot of excellent resources dedicated to this topic that I would encourage you to explore if this is a particular area of struggle for you.

It may (or may not) surprise you to learn that arguably the most influential man who ever walked the face of the earth (Jesus) struggled with this too. There is a rather obscure and even pedestrian passage that describes this dilemma. Jesus, at the peak of earthy ministry, is traveling from town to town (on foot, of course) preaching the good news and healing people. When the general population began to realize that he would feed them and could heal their sick children, they followed him around like the paparazzi! Jesus was the original rock star.

As he was preparing to move on to another city, he snuck out of the house to spend some time alone in prayer. The crowd followed him.[16] They begged him to stay in their town, but he explained that his mission was to spread the good news of the kingdom of God to other towns too. And he left.

What just happened here? Jesus essentially said to them, "Sorry, but I can't help you." He knew that there would be a mother waking up soon to realize that her terminally ill child would probably die because Jesus wasn't there to heal her. He knew that the men who thought he was there to liberate them from the oppressive Roman government might think that he was a fraud. It could not have been easy—even for the Son of God—to walk away from helpless, abandoned, destitute people who so badly needed his help.

Why didn't Jesus stay up until 2:00 a.m. to heal them and rise again at 4:30 a.m. to get everything ready so that he could still leave town the next day? That's what some of us would do. I can't know for certain, but my guess is that Jesus told them no because he was physically and emotionally spent. Look at his schedule over the past few months: Jesus went without food for forty days, came face-to-face with pure evil, was rejected by his own family, took a very long road trip, fought with some evil spirits, and healed tons of people. I don't think it's a far stretch to believe that he was introvert and needed time by himself to regroup. Jesus understood that he was human and subject to the same limitations we are, and that he didn't have limitless energy.

So the next time you ask, *What would Jesus do?*, realize that he would—and did when he walked the earth—help when he could, but he also recognized when he needed to walk away.

Know the Difference

If we are going to truly Live Free, we have to learn to control what we can control and let go of the rest. Is seems easy enough, but it's not.

Are you familiar with the Serenity Prayer?

> God, grant me the serenity to accept the
> things I cannot change,
> Courage to change the things I can,
> And wisdom to know the difference.[17]

Some of our greatest frustration and anxiety come when we can't tell the difference. We make ourselves sick worrying about the choices of others: a spouse, a child, or a parent. But truth be told, we do know the difference; the problem is that we don't want to admit it. We think we know (and sometimes we even do know) what's best for those we care about. We spend grave amounts of energy thinking of ways to make them, or at least encourage them, to do what we think needs done. At our best we seek to influence them, but at our worst we try to manipulate them.

Sometimes this concern is valid. For example, if my husband is sick and refuses to go to the doctor, I will do everything in my power to encourage him to take care of himself. I hate to see him in pain and know that the doctor can help him. And, let's face it, since we don't live on our own little islands, other people's choices affect us. I know that if he can't work, it will put an unnecessary burden on the rest of the family. Is it that selfish to look out for our own interests too?

No, it's not. But the problem is that it doesn't matter what we think. All the thinking in the world (and even begging) isn't going to get the job done, because it's not our decision. Often, we abdicate the responsibility for the things that are truly in our control and spend precious energy seeking to manipulate others to come around to our way of thinking.

This doesn't mean that we should stop showing care and concern for others. But if we are truly concerned for the well-being of our friends and loved ones, it is critical that we learn to not interfere with their "process." They, too, are independent contractors and must learn to take full responsibility for their actions. We can express concern and offer suggestions, but we can't make them see the light.

What exactly is inside our sphere of control? The answer is…not much and everything, all at the same time. We are responsible for everything in our lives—whether we caused it or not. But our circle of control can be rather small. Basically, all we have complete control over is our motives, attitudes, and actions.[18] So if I were to follow my own advice, the next time I am frustrated that my husband is not taking caring care of his health, I should go run on the treadmill to make sure that I'm taking care of my own (smile).

This may seem like an oversimplification of a complex problem, and it is. At the same time, it's very powerful to come to grips with what we can and cannot control, and then act on what we can.

The Wrap-Up

Living Free means that we must learn how to offensively control and defensively protect our own battlespace (i.e., our mind). This sometimes means saying no, even to well-meaning friends and family. Chaos will ensue if we don't properly manage what is inside our circle of control and learn to let the rest go.

Happy Is Just a Meal

The Key to Contentment

I hate to lose—it really annoys me. To borrow Billy Beane's line from the movie *Money Ball*, "I hate to lose more than I like to win." Much to my dismay, I was always a below-average athlete, so I've had to find other outlets for my competitiveness. One time at the gym, I was on the Stairmaster racing the poor unsuspecting man on the machine beside me. He stopped after reaching ninety-eight floors because he had concluded his twenty-minute workout, and I thought, *Seriously? Who stops that close to reaching a hundred floors?* Needless to say, he didn't win that day.

Do you know what depresses many of us more than losing? Winning. Yes, it's sad but true. Following the Rio Olympics in 2016, many of the athletes experienced an emotional crash that psychologist Scott Goldman, director of the Performance Psychology Center at the University of Michigan, describes as an "under-recovery." This is to be expected for those who invested endless hours training and preparing, only to fall short of their goals. But I was surprised to learn (actually, not really) that the winners[19] were equally subject to these same feelings of despair. You may have experienced a similar drop in mood after achieving a major milestone like getting married, receiving a raise, or buying a new car.

There is an obsession in our culture with happiness. I see articles, blogs, and books just about every day about how to find happiness and keep it. With all of the focus given to it, you would think that more us would enjoy all of life's pleasures to their fullest. Yet, it is estimated that at least one third of adults in North American experience anxiety or other unwellness issues.[20] It seems to me that the more we talk about how to be happy, the less of it we are.

Let's face it, as human beings we are terrible at predicting what makes us happy.

One of the reasons for this is what I consider to be a very distorted and flawed view of good and bad. We project that if we receive enough good things and avoid the bad things, we'll be happy. For example, most of us would agree that winning the lottery is good and a traumatic spinal cord injury is bad. You may be surprised to learn that ten years after either the perceived positive event or negative event, the quality of life of paraplegic victims was significantly higher than those individuals who won the lottery! Even in the months directly following the referenced events, the accident victims still reported higher levels of general happiness than the winners.[21]

As much as I hate to accept it, getting what I want does not typically make me happy. I think this is true for most of us. If it did, there would be no such thing as buyer's remorse, depressed millionaires, or spoiled brats. Getting what we want can actually make us unhappy. A study of adults who were overindulged as children showed that every single one who participated in the study reported lower self-esteem as the result of being spoiled as children. In fact, the more they were overindulged, the worse they felt about themselves as an adult.[22]

The strange irony is that getting handed what we *don't* want often illuminates the path to greater contentment and fulfillment than we could ever receive from having our wish list met. The happiest, most successful people I know are those who have overcome extremely difficult situations, not typically those who have been handed millions of dollars with no strings attached. This conclusion flies in the face of conventional wisdom. And yet, said no one ever, *If only I could lose my job, or my husband would leave me for another woman, or my plane would be hijacked today.* Even if we knew that positive outcomes would result from negative events, we still wouldn't want to experience them.

Happiness is a funny thing. It makes me happy to fill up cart my cart at TJMaxx with new shoes, but as soon as I get them to my closest (to hide them from my husband), the feeling fades. When our two older kids went through boot camp with the Air Force, they both said that the best part of their day was the *anticipation* of getting a letter during mail call. The excitement went away quickly because the fulfillment wasn't in reading the letter; it was only in the anticipation of getting one.

Is there really a way to sustain that happy feeling? I think that the Creator of the universe intended something much greater for us than bursts of euphoria generated by the release of dopamine, serotonin, oxytocin, and endorphins. He wants us to be content, even in extremely difficult situations.[23] Even though *contentment* is defined in most dictionaries as a synonym to *happiness*, I think it conveys a slightly different meaning. In my own words, contentment is the peaceful feeling we have when we realize that, after I've done everything I can do, and even if life isn't going as planned, God is still in control and I'm going to be ok.

As hard as it may be to conceive that we could experience peace and even feelings of happiness after suffering a traumatic injury or a devastating loss of a loved one, the truth is that contentment is a by-product of hard work, good choices, and God's grace. Happiness was never intended to the be the end game.

Keys to Contentment

So if happiness isn't the immediate goal, what can we do to the develop lasting, sustainable happiness that we refer to as contentment? This is not by any means an exhaustive list, but we'll discuss three keys below.

1. Work hard toward your goals.

For reasons I will never fully understand, achievement has become a dirty word in our culture. We don't want to win because it may make someone else feel badly that they lost. We don't want to post rankings because someone might be mad that they didn't perform as well (even though they didn't work as hard those who did). This mentality has fed the entitlement phenomenon and stands to rob us and our children from the happiness and fulfillment that comes from working toward—not just accomplishing—our goals.

I'm not certain what the hard-and-fast science is behind it, but I can tell you from my own personal experience that I am happiest when I am working tirelessly to fulfill my established goals using my God-given talents and abilities. I've noticed that I can even feel depressed if I'm not working hard enough to reach a goal. In my own life, boredom is the greatest cause of unhappiness.

Professional cyclist Lance Armstrong, when asked by Jeff Hayden, author of *The Motivation Myth*, what he missed most about racing said, "I don't really miss the result. I miss the work."[24]

And even when I'm successful, as with the Olympic athletes as mentioned above, I often experienced a letdown from completing the task. You may have noticed that letdown after graduating from college, buying a house, or achieving any other goal that you've worked hard toward. It's very common to hear athletes and coaches talk about feeling depressed the day after the season ends—even if they've won the Super Bowl!

2. Intentionally do things that make you unhappy in the moment...

...if they promise a greater outcome later. This is also known as discipline. My father was the most disciplined individual I had ever met. His daily regimens were so well ordered that he was often accused (and rightly so) of being inflexible. In addition to a daily time of prayer and Bible reading, he journaled regularly and worked out religiously. He was very structured with his eating habits as well. Once when we were younger, after reading a book about the harmful effects of refined white sugar on the body, he banned ice cream from the house, an act for which we still haven't forgiven him!

He made it clear to us from a young age that it wasn't his job as our father to make us happy; it was his job to raise us to fear God (i.e., respect God) and be self-sufficient, productive members of society. He knew that if he and my mother were successful with those objectives, the rest would fall into place. This was exasperating at times growing up, but his focus on living a disciplined life has paid big dividends in my life.

3. Do the right thing, even if it costs you.

As a culture, we have rejected the concept of absolute truth. We are so afraid that we might be perceived as judgmental that we buy into the idea that there is no right and no wrong; everyone gets to choose their own version of the truth. We have all heard it: *What might be right for you may not be right for me.* But is that really the way it works?

No, it isn't.

A few weeks ago, friends had given us tickets to go to the Steelers game. The seats were amazing, and the weather was beautiful. It was a great night. There was a festival going on in the city that week, so there were vendor trucks lined up outside the gate as we left the game. After ordering our very overpriced ice cream ($14 for the two of us), the young woman handed my husband change from his $20 bill. I was so wrapped up in my hot fudge sundae that I didn't notice that she gave him $16 in change. Perry noticed, however, and handed her back the extra $10 bill she had given him. She thanked him, and we headed to our car. Perry made an enlightening comment to me as we were walking through the parking lot: "I want to be able to sleep tonight." Though he had $10 less in his pocket, he slept like a baby that night because he knew what was right, and he did it.

It's not always easy to know what's right. This particular story seems pretty straightforward, but it's not. Many of us would be able to justify why we needed that $10 more than the store owner. Or, we could justify that the prices were inflated and our purchase really wasn't worth that much money. Our choices can become very cloudy when we make up the rules as we go along.

The terrorists who flew passenger jets into buildings in New York City on September 11, 2001, were convinced that were doing the right thing according to Allah.

The loyal followers of Jim Jones who "drank the Kool-Aid" and died in the 1978 mass murder-suicide in Guyana, South America were sincerely dedicated to making the world a better place. [25]

Kathi Aultman, the former abortion doctor turned pro-life, testified before Congress in support of the Heartbeat Bill that for years she held the view that it was "wrong to bring unwanted children into an over populated world" and felt she was performing a valuable service. It wasn't until much later that she realized that she was killing human beings.[26]

Young lieutenants in Nazi Germany's Third Reich considered themselves to be good soldiers by following the orders of their superiors, only later to be tried and convicted as war criminals.

Some of the greatest atrocities known to mankind have been committed when individuals or cultures bought into the idea that the rules of morality can be adjusted based on circumstance. The misguided, and often downright evil, concept that truth is subjective has provided the perfect guise for the strong to exploit the weak throughout the ages.

Do you want to sleep better at night? Abide by the moral code. Notice that I didn't say "a" moral code. We didn't make the rules and we don't get to change them. God laid out the ground rules for mankind when He created the universe, and He's the only one with the authority to change them. We can take the Ten Commandments off the wall of our court rooms and schools, but we can't erase the laws written on our hearts.[27] Our consciences didn't get the memo that the rules have changed.

The reason that people *think* the rules have changed, however, is because our culture has done a stellar job of separating choices from consequences. For example, it was my spouse's fault that our marriage failed. Or, I lost my job because my boss is a jerk. If we refuse to acknowledge that our own poor choices are causing this dilemma, then the mess we're in cannot be our fault. To carry it a step further, if it's not my fault, then I am the victim and someone else is responsible to fix it: my parents, my spouse, the school system, or the government.

Are you familiar with the song "It Ain't My Fault" by Brothers Osborne? It's written about a young man who goes to a place he knows he shouldn't be, drinks more than he knows he should, gets in a fight because he says something he shouldn't have said, and ends up in bed with someone he didn't walk in with. Despite all of this, he declares very boldly that it's not his fault. He goes to such great lengths to point out how everyone and everything else is at fault for his actions that it's clear that the songwriter is mocking him.

Further complicating the issue is the fact that consequences are often delayed. If we don't get caught immediately and must pay the price, we can be lulled into thinking that we got away with something. But rest assured that there are always consequences to our actions—both good and bad—even if we don't see them immediately.

The Wrap-Up

We will get better at predicting what makes us happy when we understand that working toward our goals, and not just achieving them, is often more fulfilling. Happiness comes to disciplined individuals who understand how to achieve their goals, rather than spoiled children who get everything they want.

If you want to experience happiness and contentment in your life, avoid the trap of thinking that laws of morality don't apply to you and learn to follow your conscience. God has wired us to know right from wrong. How to do this would be an entire book on its own, but the first step is to accept that there is objective truth and to commit yourself to following it. It would be accurate to say that this is not always exciting or sexy, but living by the moral code will bring you great happiness and contentment.

Don't Unpack Your Bags

The Key to Becoming Resilient

Two friends come to mind as I write about resilience. My friend Terri is married to a wonderful man, has two amazing daughters, and lives in a beautiful home in the suburbs of Pittsburgh. She is well educated and had a very lucrative job working for a large corporation. Aside from some minor ailments, she has enjoyed good health for all her adult life.

I love her dearly, but I cannot figure out why Terri is so unhappy. She quit her job several years ago to pursue other interests but doesn't appear to be involved in anything and spends a lot of time at home by herself. I've known Terri for a long time, and I'm not aware of any unusual situations or events that would have caused her to want to isolate herself.

My other friend, Tammy, also is well educated, has a wonderful husband, and lives in a nice home. She sings in the worship band at church and is very engaged in the community. Tammy has a contagious smile and a very kind spirit. Many people, including myself, are naturally drawn to her because of her positive outlook on life and enjoy spending as much time with her as our schedules allow.

You would never know from meeting Tammy that she and her husband tragically lost both of their children before they could reach the age of adulthood. Matthew was born with a rare form of dwarfism. He was one of four living children with this condition, but that wasn't the reason he died. Matthew died at the age of two from a fever after developing an ear infection. His fever spiked so high that it caused brain damage, and ultimately his death.

They also have a beautiful daughter named Alex, who is now is heaven with Matthew. She went to high school with my older children and was born one day before my daughter, Valerie. Alex was a cheerleader and part of a competitive gymnastics team in our area. She died in a one-car accident a few years ago. She was driving home from her boyfriend's house on a week night in November of her senior year. Her car struck the only tree on that side of the road. Emergency responders speculated that a deer ran out in front of her, but this was—and still is—another unexplained tragedy. Coincidently, Tammy's husband lost his job the day before the accident. Talk about adding insult to injury.

I know that these two brief paragraphs don't do justice to Tammy's story (used with permission, of course), but I couldn't imagine talking about resiliency and how it is possible to become healthy and whole again after tragedy without thinking of her. She is truly a remarkable individual and has taught me so much.

Fortunately, most of us never experience an earthshaking event of this magnitude, but we all face setbacks and disappointments. Often, it's hard to tell if someone will be resilient after experiencing a trauma or setback, because both groups of people experience the same emotions…at least initially. Why is it that some of us can survive—even thrive—after earth-shaking events like these, and others of us are paralyzed by fear and anxiety by much lesser challenges?

It's perfectly normal, and even healthy, to experience the full range of emotions when faced with disappointing or distressing situations. You may remember the five stages of grief: denial, anger, bargaining, depression, and acceptance.[28] The problem isn't when we experience the phases; it's when we don't progress through them. Of course, there is no time limit to grief, but the grieving period should be proportionate to the loss. And no one but you can measure the magnitude of these events on your life. Some events are so intense that they are what we call "game-changers." The loss of a spouse or child is a game-changer. The grief may never completely go away. A debilitating injury is also a game-changer. Many are never able to go back to normal activities. Those closest to you may want you to "get over it" much quicker than is comfortable for you, but you don't have to follow anyone else's timetable. You just have to keep moving forward.

Remember this: you can visit, but you can't live there. Don't unpack your bags because you don't want to live there. It's no fun. Change is inevitable. Loss is a natural part of the fallen human condition. Even healthy, vibrant organisms will die if they stagnate. But as counterintuitive as it seems, the happiest, most successful people I know are those who have overcome extreme—even devastating—circumstances to find themselves stronger and healthier, and more resilient than ever before.

This is not a natural process, however. Do you remember what I wrote earlier, that we always have a choice as to how we respond to our environments? You have probably heard the expression "that which doesn't kill you makes you stronger."[29] To be candid, that's a lie. It's not in our nature to take pain and hardship, and learn from it. It always—and I mean, always—requires tough choices on our part. This is why two people can be involved in the same accident, or go through the same divorce, or suffer from the same devastating illness, and yet experience very different outcomes.

Shania Twain was twenty-one when her mother and stepfather were killed in a head-on car accident. She had to put her career on hold to care for her younger teenaged siblings and didn't head to Nashville until her youngest brother graduated from high school. She didn't permit her grief to render her helpless or hopeless.

Tyler Perry was physically and sexually abused growing up. He was kicked out of high school and tried to commit suicide twice. In a desperate attempt to get his career moving, he put all of his savings into a show that failed miserably. He didn't allow abuse or failure to define him as an individual and control his future.[30]

Bethany Hamilton was thirteen when she suffered a near-fatal shark attack that resulted in the loss of her left arm. She was back on a surfboard within a month, then won first place in the Explorer Women's Division of the NSSA National Championships two years later.[31] She didn't let fear paralyze her, even though no one would have blamed her if she did.

There is no simple process for overcoming tragedy and setbacks, but resilient individuals like the ones mentioned above have provided clues for us:

1. Pray for God's supernatural strength and wisdom.

You can't do it alone. The most resilient people I know (and know of) have a deep relationship with Jesus as the Lord and Savior of their lives. This is no coincidence. All those mentioned above who have triumphed over extreme heartbreak and loss have publicly acknowledged their commitment to God and recognized his supernatural help. God is the very definition of hope when we are in impossible and desperate situations. He is close to the heartbroken, is the father of the fatherless, is always with us to help us, gives us the strength to accomplish even the most difficult tasks, and provides for our every need out of His great wealth.[32-36]

Why would anyone choose to go through this life without God's wisdom, comfort, and help? Personally, I'll never understand that. Our ego, maybe? The cost associated with following Jesus? Possibly. And yes, there is a cost. But the choices we make in difficult times, including the one to put aside our pride and ask for Divine help, will decide whether we will be defined by fear or faith.

2. Recognize what you may have gained as a result of the loss.

My mom observed recently that with every loss there is something we gain too. It seems counterintuitive, but it's true. There is always something that we have after a loss or traumatic event that we didn't have before: new relationships, new freedom, or new influence.

When we spend our time fixated on how this could happen we get stuck in denial and lose sight of how this tragedy could provide renewed purpose in our life. My friend Linda always says, *"Our pain is our platform."* After experiencing a very painful divorce from her unfaithful husband, Linda uses what she has learned as an opportunity to help other women in her situation. My friend Tammy, mentioned above, has helped so many hurting and grieving people that she would not have been able to help without a new perspective.

Granted, these gains are not always things that we would have asked for or wanted. And yet, they prove to be powerful tools to help the grieving process and become an integral part of who we are.

3. Take out your aggression in a productive way.

Anger is an undeniable part of the grieving process. As much as we would like to knock someone's lights out at times, like a scene from a *Rocky* movie, "that won't solve anything" (as mom used to say). When we experience stress, hormones are released in our bodies that cause blood vessels to constrict, and more oxygen is sent to the muscles in case we need unusual strength in order to act. This is known as the flight or fight response. This is why we can become aggressive when we're angry. All of that extra energy needs to go somewhere.

We all understand how trauma impacts our brain and emotions, but we don't often realize the physiological effect on our bodies. The increase in heart rate and blood pressure will, over time, put excessive stress on our cardiovascular system, which could cause a heart attack or stroke. If that excessive oxygen and blood flow isn't managed productively, we will lash out aggressively or pay a price for it in our physical health.

This is precisely why exercise is so critical to our emotional health, not just our physical health. Exercise releases endorphins, which trigger happy feelings. In fact, many mental health experts are convinced that exercise is more effective in treating anxiety and depression than any medications on the market today. Aerobic, or sustained exercise of medium to high intensity, is an excellent way to process the excessive oxygen levels and messy chemicals released into our systems as a result of stress.

My father died on December 9, 2016, at the age of seventy-four. My dad wasn't your typical septuagenarian, and this was a tremendous shock to all of us. He still operated his own accounting business, lifted weights religiously three times a week, and had just put away his Harley Davidson Heritage Softail for the winter. Only three years prior to this, he was involved in a serious motorcycle accident where he broke bones in his neck, back, and pelvis. Not only did he survive, but he also recovered well enough to ride again! I love to tell the story that he purchased his next motorcycle while still in a wheelchair and headed to the gym with his granddaughter on his way home from the doctor's office after he was cleared to take off the neck brace. He was one tough cookie. He survived this near-fatal accident only to die of a lung infection from pneumonia. This is just one of the many things I'll never understand this side of heaven.

After leaving the hospital for the final time and grabbing something to eat, my brothers, our kids, and I headed to the gym. It was our way of honoring Dad, because that's where he would have gone that day if the situation were reversed. It also helped us all to work out our frustration, anger, and sadness. In fact, during the previous week and a half while Dad was in a coma, my younger brother and I headed to the gym every afternoon after visiting the hospital. This was our way of coping. Working out was a great way to clear our minds so that we could prepare for the difficult days ahead.

It's so important at stressful times to do something productive with that pent-up energy. If not, we may act on our negative thoughts and feelings in ways we will later regret. Once we flip off the boss, or post nasty things on Twitter, or punch out an in-law, we can't put the "toothpaste back in the tube," as they say.

4. Accept the new normal and move forward.

Just months after her daughter, Alex, died, Tammy agreed to lead a small group of teenage girls as part of our church's youth group. Many of them were classmates of Alex (imagine that). Even though Tammy was able to hold it together at the Tuesday evening groups, she admits that every week she sobbed all the way home. As painful as it was, though, she knew that giving back to others and serving a purpose was an important part of her healing. Because she pushed through the pain, she didn't allow herself to remain stuck in her grief.

She still misses her children desperately, but she does not allow her pain to control her life or threaten her relationships, particularly her marriage. Brian processed his grief differently but achieved the same result: wholeness and relative happiness after such a great loss. Because both Tammy and Brian were able to push forward through the pain, they were able to preserve their marriage, against overwhelmingly unfavorable odds.

The Wrap-Up

Simply put, there are times when life just sucks. Death, tragedy, and loss are part of the fallen condition of humanity. To Live Free mean that we experience the full range of emotions, but we don't allow our grief or sadness to be so overwhelming that it defines who we are as individuals. It's not the event, but our capacity to be resilient—to become strong again after bad things happen—that will determine our future.

But make no mistake about it, the struggle is real. Your pain is real. For every success story there are a million others who drown their sorrow in alcohol and wind up in rehab, or act out in rage and land in jail, or refuse to forgive or let go and remain trapped in a prison of their own making.

If it were easy to be resilient, we would all do it, but you've got this. Don't allow your pain and loss to chart the course for your future. God created you, loves you, and has a plan and purpose for your life.[37] He not only heals our pain, but He redeems it and assigns purpose to it.

Don't unpack your bags, because you're just passing through.

Be an Average Parent

The Key to Raising Resilient Children

My grandmother Rose Collura, my mom's mom, was born in 1911 to immigrant parents. She was the oldest of five children. When her mother was in her early thirties, she died suddenly, leaving Rose the unenviable responsibility of caring for her younger siblings. Rose was twelve years old when she became the primary caregiver in her household. The worst part of this new role for her was that she had to quit school because her youngest sister was only an infant at the time. I remember her telling me stories about how she used to stand at the front door and cry when she sent the older kids off to school because she couldn't go.

And yet, as an adult she not only ran a successful business—she ran two! She and Angelo, my grandfather, bought a building that housed a small grocery store and a bar room with a small apartment on the second floor. My grandfather operated the bar side, but Rose handled the bookkeeping and ordered inventory for both businesses. They supported all three of my grandmother's sisters until they were married and could support themselves. My mother still remembers when all seven of them lived together in that tiny two-bedroom apartment. And Rose engineered all of that with only a sixth grade education.

That was a different time, wasn't it?

The good news is, we've come a long way since the Great Depression era, and our children will never be in a situation where they would need to overcome such insurmountable circumstances. The bad news is, I'm not convinced that they could.

Our newfound prosperity in this country has created an entirely new set of problems. During my grandmother's era, great parents were ones who could feed their children, provide a roof over their heads, and make sure that they had the opportunity to graduate from high school. Now we're obsessed with providing every opportunity for our children to get ahead in an extremely competitive environment: for colleges, for teams, and for jobs.

The bar has risen with parenting. And yet our children struggle with anxiety and depression more than ever. As our ability to provide for our children rises, their ability to cope with life's challenges falls.

So how do we as parents provide the best for our kids without compromising their ability to fend for themselves? While I'm not completely out of the woods yet as a parent (we still have a sixteen-year-old son at home), I would say that I've discovered the secret to raising healthy, resilient children: being an average parent.

Of course, I'm not advocating being abusive or neglectful in any way. We average parents love our kids as much as everyone else. But as I learned from my father, it isn't my job to make my kids happy; it is my job to raise them to be independent, productive members of society. To do that means that sometimes they aren't going to like me, and I am never going to be up for the parent of the year award.

All the things we want to protect our kids from, and those things we even feel it's our job to shield them from—

pain, frustration, embarrassment, confusion, and even basic needs such as hunger—are the very struggles that create healthy adults who can fight for themselves. But admittedly, allowing our kids to deal with problems on their own, or even refrain from doing everything in our power to give them the advantage as students or athletes can make us look like bad parents.

For example, when our son was fifteen years old, he was working at a restaurant washing dishes three miles from our house. One day in late October, I was on my way home from my job, so that I could take him to work, but there was a communication glitch. Even though I would have been home on time to take him, I had no way to get a hold of him. Rather inconveniently, our house phone was down at the time and his cell phone had broken the week before.

When I got home, I saw a note on the table that said, *Mom, no one was here to take me to work so I rode my bike. Oh, my goodness, I thought, what if he gets in an accident? Or what if the neighbors see that I made Nick ride his bike to work on this cold, rainy day?*

But hours later when I knew that he had arrived safely and after I got over my embarrassment, I realized something: he was extremely proud of himself. He told that story for months to anyone who would listen. Nick is not at all shy, so that added up to a large pool of people. It's interesting to note that he received one or both of the following comments from just about every adult to whom he recounted the story: They either gave him their phone number in case he needed a ride in the future (which he took a couple of them up on their offer), or they told him to come back and see them when he got out of school and they would give him a job!

As counterintuitive as it seems, it's those very things that do not give you the warm fuzzy feelings about being a great parent that can be the most beneficial in developing all of those necessary traits that lead to exceptional adults.

To name a few:

- Creating and enforcing a curfew
- Saying no – *No, you can't go to that party; no, sorry, we can't go on vacation this year; no, I can't give you money for gas.*
- Sending your teenaged daughter back to change her clothes, even if it means that she will miss her ride and have to take the bus
- Having difficult conversations about drugs, sex, and relationships

If you start to question if you are a terrible parent, it's possible that you're on the right track. We have worked so hard to give our kids everything that we didn't have that we forget to give them the things that we did have.

I would like to highlight three things that average parents need to give and three things we need to withhold:

Three Things Your Children Need

1. Your time

It sounds easy enough, but it's not. We have an abundance of everything these days, except time. To further complicate this issue, as our kids get older, they don't even want us around. I was a stay-at-home mom until my oldest was almost 18. I remember him and his sister begging me to get a job so that we could go on vacation and buy better hockey equipment.

When our youngest was in first grade, I went back to work full-time so that my husband could start his own business. We finally had more money for "stuff," but this created a new set of challenges. This change in employment for both of us forced a shift in family responsibilities as well. We received healthcare benefits from my employer, but the job was over forty-five minutes from home and kept me away for nearly eleven hours a day. As a result, Perry took on the shopping, cooking, and the responsibility for getting Nick on and off of the school bus. Needless to say, after being home for the previous seventeen years and being responsible for making dinner every night, I *loved* going back to work.

Two years into this process, I heard Nick tell another adult that he was being raised by his father! That was crushing. I remember thinking, *You've got to be kidding me.* I was home with this kid from the time he was born until he was old enough to go to school, but Dad was now the parent of choice and I was chopped liver.

But even when they don't want us around, the time, attention, and affection that we give our kids during their developmental years are invaluable toward developing strong adults.

2. Your supervision

Psychologists have discovered that children perceive monitoring as a way of showing care and affection.[38] As much as our children pretend that they hate it when we tell them no, listen to what your son says the next time you tell him that he can't go somewhere with his friend. If the conversations in your house are anything like the conversations in my house, your child will say, "But Danny is allowed to go. HIS PARENTS DON'T CARE." They hate us because we don't allow them to do everything they want to do, even though they know in the back of their minds that they shouldn't be doing them. If you think about, our kids are paying us a backhanded compliment when they get mad for being told no.

A very tragic example of lack of supervision gone wrong was Eric Harris, one of the shooters at Columbine High School in 1999. When the police searched the Harris house after the shooting, they found a shotgun, shells, and a bomb in his bedroom. Apparently, his mother never ventured into his room during the six months he was plotting the attack.[39]

3. Yourself—unfiltered

As difficult as it is, it's important that our children see our flaws and observe the good, the bad, and the ugly. Let them see how you deal with difficult family members, money problems, neighbors, etc.

Resist the temptation to be "perfect." Some of us find that easier to do than others. My twenty-four-year old daughter, Val, reminded me just recently that we made her and her older brother buy their lunches at school once they turned sixteen and started working. Money was so tight at that time in our lives that our options were limited and we needed them to pitch in. Although I'm not proud of that, I know of parents who would go into debt before they would allow their children to know they were struggling to pay the bills.

When you are fighting the urge to put on a front for your children, remember this: perfect parents create anxious kids.[40]

Three Things Your Children Don't Need

1. Some of their wants

Parenting experts say that accommodating our children's every need will actually fuel anxiety. "Whenever we try to provide certainty and comfort, we are getting in the way of children being able to develop their own problem-solving and mastery."[41] For example, making sure that you arrive at the school fifteen minutes early so that your child won't have to wait for you can backfire. What happens when one day, because of circumstances outside of your control, you're late? They panic.

2. Some of the answers

Val was always the one who liked to work with my husband on home-improvement projects. She was thirteen years old when Perry was gutting the lathe and plaster from the living room of our old farm house. My husband would rip it out and dump it outside the window into the wheel barrel. Val's job was to take the full wheel barrel and dump it over the hill. She commented that it was really heavy, but it wasn't until much later that Perry noticed that the wheel on the wheel barrel was completely deflated! She had been dragging 100 lb. loads across the yard for three hours using a defective piece of equipment. But she figured it out, nonetheless.

It's my personal observation that providing our kids with state-of-the-art sports equipment, for example, at no personal expense (to them, not us) robs them of the creativity and resourcefulness they will need when starting families of their own with limited resources.

3.   Only some of the risks

I saw a segment on the news a few months ago about Dump Adventure Playgrounds. This concept was first developed after World War II when sociologists were studying the impact of war and found kids happily playing on the mounds of rubble.[42] This idea was first brought to the US in the 1970s, but lost popularity due to rising safety concerns.

This brand of playground has resurfaced in New York in the past few years because researchers are starting to realize the tremendous impact that this form of unstructured, uninhibited play has on intellectual, social, and physical development. These playgrounds are home to old tires, planks of wood, nails, saws, hammers, drills, and other junk that children could use to construct their own masterpieces. They also come equipped with "playworkers" to supervise since there is a strict no-parent rule.

What is even more remarkable than the fact that parents are allowing their children to play under such dangerous conditions is the discovery that many of the safety concerns may be unwarranted. "In every study that I've found that has been done, adventure playgrounds have much lower levels of serious injury than your sort have much lower levels of serious injury than your sort of traditional playgrounds," said Reilly Wilson, graduate student for the Children's Environments Research Group, focusing on adventure playgrounds. "Part of it is that regular playgrounds, as it were, are designed for safety and young people know that. So when young people play on a regular playground, they often pay less attention to risks."[43]

The Wrap-Up

It's important for us to recognize that our job as parents is not to protect our child from every risk but to give them the skills they need to know in order to protect themselves. And then when necessary, we can teach them how to pick up the pieces and move forward.

Don't Overaccessorize

The Key to Eliminating Unproductive Guilt

A woman walked into to my friend Sarah's counseling office, took off her shoes, and sat on the couch. This was unusual that a client would make herself that comfortable on the first visit. She proceeded to tell Sarah about an event that happened when she was in her twenties. She was planning a birthday party for a brother, which happened to be the same day that her father was scheduled to run a leg of the city's marathon with a team of co-workers. At his daughter's request, the father switched his section of the relay to earlier in the day so that he could make the party scheduled for later that afternoon. Her father had just completed a half-mile hill, and as he approached his daughter, who was waiting for him at the relay point, he dropped dead from a heart attack.

She conveyed to Sarah that she believed her father would still be alive if she hadn't asked him to change the leg of his relay. Now, over thirty years later, this woman was still holding on to guilt over her father's death.

Guilt is so common that I compare it to just another accessory that we carry with us everywhere we go. For women, it's like a purse or scarf; for men, it's like a belt around their waist. We just can't leave home without it. We wear that guilt like it's our job and would feel naked without it. Sometimes, we have our guilt under control and we're able to hide it in the form of a small handbag or a tasteful belt buckle. There are other times when the guilt is so big and so loud that it overpowers us. We allow it to define us, as was the case with the woman mentioned above.

Unwarranted guilt can be a very destructive force in our lives because it steals our joy and diverts our attention from what is most important. If not properly understood and processed, guilt can render us helpless.

Not All Guilt Is Bad

Whether we realize it or not, guilt—like most emotions—serves a purpose in the human experience. The pain that we experience when we "feel guilty" is a warning signal that something is off balance. In the same way that physical pain is an indication of a problem in our body, guilt can be an indication of a threat to our physical, emotional, and spiritual well-being.

It's important to understand that pain is not the enemy. Pain of all types is designed to alert us to the potential problem. In 2012, at the age of fifty-one, my husband experienced a life-threatening heart event. This was a very scary situation, but because of the quick and skilled reaction by the paramedics (and the grace of God) he is still alive today. When I tell people about his heart attack, the most typical response is, "Oh, how terrible!" But it really wasn't. The heart attack was the best thing that could have happened, because it brought the problem to light so that he could get the help he needed. Only hours after the doctors implanted two stints in his artery he felt worlds better.

I know it sounds like I'm splitting hairs, but the heart attack was not the problem; his blocked artery was the problem. The heart event, though precarious and painful, was the best thing that happened, because it called attention to the true problem…before it was too late.

In the same way, guilt is a warning that something isn't lining up with our belief system. Think of it as one of those annoying alerts that we get on our cell phone warning us of potentially destructive weather in our area. Sometimes the threat is real and sometimes it's not. In January of 2018, an emergency alert was accidentally sent out to over a million cell phones that a ballistic missile was headed toward one of the Hawaiian Islands.[44] Obviously (thank God!), that was a false alarm. The point is that we shouldn't ignore guilt; we just need to process it properly.

In order to properly deal with guilt, there are times when we need to adjust our behavior, and then there are times when we need to adjust our belief system. There are three steps we should follow to properly assess which direction we should take.

1. Recognize what is causing the feelings of guilt.

Did you ever have that nagging feeling that something isn't right? If you are alive and breathing, I'm guessing that you have. As mentioned above, most of us would think something is wrong if we didn't feel that way. (Can you see the problem here?) When I sense that something is "off," I try to evaluate why. Sometimes that nagging feeling is a reminder that I haven't eaten all day. Unfortunately, this scenario doesn't happen as often as I would like. Because our mind, soul, and spirit are so closely connected, isolating the problem can be difficult.

But more often than not, the relentless nagging in my mind is because of something I said or did. In my personal experience, there are several different sources of guilt:

- I did something, or considered doing something, intentionally that violated my conscience (such as cheating on my taxes).

- I said something that I knew could be offensive. I should have just let it go, but I said it anyway (such as calling out a co-worker for not doing his job).

- I said or did something that, even though my intensions were pure, was misconstrued or caused offense (such as offering help to someone who didn't want it).

- I disappointed someone who was counting on me (such as missing my son's baseball game because I stayed late at work or forgetting a commitment that I had previously made).

- I did something that didn't align with my stated goal of losing weight and being healthy (such as eating that chocolate cake last night or binge-watching episodes on Netflix instead of writing this chapter).

- I failed to do something that someone, somewhere probably thought I should have done.

- I breathed the wrong way.

OK, maybe not the last one, but you get the idea.

The first step to productively processing guilt is to understand the source, which sounds simple to do, but it's not.

2. Fix it or forget it.

After we have assessed the threat, we need to determine the proper course of action. Your first line of defense against guilt should be to ask yourself, *Can I do anything to correct this situation?* Sometimes we can, and sometimes we can't. There are times when the offense is so blatant and indefensible that restitution is advised.

When I was in grade school, I used to work on the weekends at my grandmother's corner grocery store. This was a small family-owned business, and my grandma appreciated the company even if I wasn't a lot of help to her. As I got older, she would allow my brothers and me to work the cash register. One day I "borrowed" money from the cash register. When my parents found out, they were livid! Not only did I need to apologize to my grandmother (who, of course, told my parents that she said I could take that money). I also needed to return the cash and offer to work extra hours at the store cleaning to compensate for my mistake. If there is a way to tangibly make up for our indiscretion that's reasonable and advisable, we should do it. But sometimes all we can do is show remorse, apologize for our actions, and move on.

Often when I commit an offense, it's because of an error in judgment and not because I intended to be malicious or cause harm. An example of this type of judgment error is an ill-advised comment. I don't think I'm the only one who ever asked another woman if she was pregnant when she wasn't. Oops. That's the type of mistake that we typically only make once.

There are other times when our actions are intended to hurt or offend, and we hit our target. Chances are, if you have a family (hint: we all do), then you have been on the giving or receiving end. While there are no hard-and-fast rules on when to apologize, if you are the offender, generally speaking now's a good time. The concept of Living Free means that we do everything in our power to live at peace with everyone.[45] Yes, even your mother-in-law. (That stereotype isn't nearly as funny now that I'm one!) We probably all know families where members have been in a ten-year standoff. Don't allow this to be your family. These untenable situations require someone to break the cycle of offense. We all know how that works: You offend me, so I offend you. Now you are doubly offended and strike back at me, and the cycle perpetuates itself. These are situations where nobody wins and everyone loses.

Every now and again you will run into a situation where you have done your level best to break the cycle and resolve the situation (even if it's not your doing), but the other side will not budge. Regardless of your effort to apologize and work through the conflict, the other party refuses to engage. As distressing as this can be, please remember: *you and I are NOT responsible for how our words are interpreted; we are only responsible for how they are intended.* If you act out of pure motives, such as care or concern for the individual, but they twist your words or actions, there is nothing you can do. The best advice I can give? Let it go. Forget about it.

Eleanor Roosevelt once said, "You wouldn't worry about what someone else thinks about you if you realized how seldom they do."[46]

3. Change your behavior or beliefs.

As mentioned at the beginning of this chapter, guilt occurs when our actions don't align with our belief system. This can work in both directions: we can believe that our actions are justified when they are not, or we can believe that because of our insatiable desire to be perfect, our actions are inexcusable when they are considered acceptable.

When to Change Your Behavior

As human beings we have a built-in, God-given sensor to alert us to trouble…also known as our conscience. Some of us have a highly developed, very sensitive conscience. I remember the first (and only time) my younger brother tried smoking when he was in middle school. He felt so guilty about it that he immediately went home and told Mom. Even though we weren't always this forthcoming about our missteps, the kids in my family knew expectations for our behavior inside and outside of the home thanks to consciences being in overdrive.

This ability to know right from wrong is more often caught than taught. And the more we listen to our conscience, the stronger it becomes. But even when our conscience is alive and well, this doesn't always mean that we follow it. We can encourage those around us—children, employees, friends— by modeling the commitment to morality, but the ultimate responsibility falls on each "independent contractor."

Even when we should know better, if we intentionally ignore our conscience repeatedly, we will no longer feel guilty when we violate our moral values. This happens often in extramarital affairs. Even though the cheating party initially feels guilty, he or she eventually rejects or denies the feelings of guilt so often that his or her conscience "breaks," similar to how our car breaks down if we repeatedly ignore the "check engine" warning signal.

This is a very dangerous place to be. Do your best to always protect your conscience. It's well established that most people who commit heinous crimes or acts of terror have either broken their conscience or adopted belief systems that support—not reject—their malicious behavior. Experts believe that the actions of terrorists, such as those who flew jet liners into the Twin Towers, aligned with their belief system. In short, they may have sincerely thought that it was the right thing to do. Their conscience was broken.

Occasionally, however, feelings of guilt can be very productive. They alert us that our behavior is not aligning with the goals that we've set for ourselves. If my goal is to run a marathon, the nagging feeling of guilt when I don't complete the ten-mile run on my training schedule is going to help keep me on track. Or, my guilty conscience for eating two pieces of cake at that party should motivate me to seriously limit my carb intake starting Monday morning. The more determined I am to reach my objectives, the stronger the sense of guilt will be when I deviate from my plan. This is one of the reasons that high achievers very commonly struggle with performance anxiety. Our guilt reflex is on steroids.

When to Change Your Beliefs

There are other times, however, when our behavior is within acceptable limits, but our belief system is out of whack. Even when I follow the diet or exercise plan or reading schedule, I'm still haunted by the feeling that I'm not doing enough. Sometimes it's a false sense of modesty that makes us feel guilty for taking credit for something we've worked very hard toward. I've talked to a lot of men who feel guilty for not being better providers for their families. There's no issue with wanting to take care of your family; in fact, this is very noble and the sign of a good husband and father. The problem comes when working fifty hours a week, owning a four-bedroom home in the suburbs, sending your children to private school, and having two late-model cars parked in the driveway still isn't enough. Instead of picking up a side job so that we can go on more vacations, we may need to adjust the thought patterns and beliefs that dictate our priorities.

We have this nagging sense that there was more that we could have done, should have done, could have anticipated, must have known, and on and on. There can be a lot of different causes for this but the most common one is our deep-seated need to be *perfect*, all of the time. This can take on a lot of different forms and shapes, but the root cause remains the same.

When conducting my own research for this chapter, I reached out to some of my younger friends to ask what it is that makes them feel guilty. One particular response stuck out to me because she said what many of us women are thinking:

> I am a guilt queen. I always feel bad about everything. Mostly I'd say I always feel like everything needs to be perfect, and if it's not, it's the worst thing in the world. I feel guilty when I

do things for myself, like reading and studying.
Then I feel guilty that I should be doing some
"stay-at-home busy work" that no one else has
time to do. I feel guilty if I don't have enough time
to do all the things that I feel need to be done or
people I need to visit. Guilt is a hard one. Good
luck writing about it, ha ha!

We could change a couple details to match our story,
but the message would be the same: I feel guilty because I'm
not perfect.

This very common but very faulty belief that we
should act, think, talk, walk, eat, sleep, work, play, perform,
parent, etc. perfectly all the time is the primary culprit to
many of our anxiety-related issues. The more we identify
ourselves as high achievers, the more we struggle with this. If
you're like me, and you rank high on the Type A personality
scale, you know exactly what I am talking about. We all know
intellectually that perfection is impossible, and yet we think
we need to hold ourselves to that standard anyway. This is
such an important topic that an entire chapter is dedicated to
it (see chapter 8: "Plan B Is the New Plan A").

Back to the story at the beginning of the chapter…

My friend Sarah was able to wisely assess the situation.
After taking some time to listen to her client's story, Sarah
stopped her to ask what share of the responsibility in his
death belonged to her father. Wow, the woman was stunned
because she had never considered that. Sarah pointed out that
he must have run past half a dozen emergency responders
on his way to the hand-off point. He had to have been in
very serious pain—possibly even for days—leading up to a
heart event of that magnitude. (I know from my husband's
experience that he had warning signs that he ignored for a
minimum of three days.) It's possible that her father made a
conscious decision to run the marathon anyway, even though

he knew something wasn't right. Even if this wasn't the case, his daughter's request to change his schedule didn't cause the heart attack—a blockage in his artery did.

The guilt that this poor woman had experienced for the last three decades (!) was the result of a faulty belief system that concluded that her event planning was somehow 100 percent responsible for her father's death. Just forty-five minutes after walking into Sarah's office for the first time, the woman replied, "Where were you thirty years ago?"

The Wrap-Up

Guilt specifically, and pain in general, is not the enemy. Emotional and physical pain are warning signs to alert us to a problem. God put mechanisms in place to protect us and not harm us. In the same way that we maintain our vehicles and other complex systems, we need to pay careful attention to our conscience to prevent it from breaking down.

Remember...your mind is the battlespace you are sworn to protect, and this is war. God has given you a sound mind to be able to discern what is true and what is false. You don't have to internalize every impulse of guilt that comes your way. Take it out, look at it, then determine if this is a warning signal to change your behavior or your beliefs.

We don't have to wear all this unhealthy guilt like it's just another part of our wardrobe. Get rid of it. Don't overaccessorize.

Plan B Is the New Plan A

The Key to Overcoming Failure

When I was in fifth grade and my brother was in fourth, my parents signed us up to play soccer for Shaler Soccer Club. It was the first year for the program, and it was kind of a big deal because we were one of the first communities in our area to have an organized soccer league. My dad was excited to get us involved since he didn't have the opportunity to play organized sports until he was older. And even though money was very tight, we could afford the $20 per child fee. He didn't have any aspirations for us to receive a full ride to college when he registered his ten- and eleven-year-old children for the season; he was just happy that we would be getting exercise.

In my generation, parents are crazy enough to pay thousands—and I mean, thousands—of dollars for their nine-year-olds to play year round and attend tournaments out of state. The main objective is no longer just exercise. This is a far cry from the $20 fee days. Our kids can't even play for a school-funded team for $20. There is no judgment here if this is you, because I've done it too. Our older kids both played hockey at the same time, and we're guilty of the above.

It's no wonder that *both* we and our children suffer from anxiety at alarming rates. We have this notion that our six-year-old is going to be the next Sydney Crosby or Matt Stafford, so we invest in the best equipment and the most elite training. So when our growing, awkward fifteen-year-old son is cut from the school football or hockey team, we both feel like failures. No pressure there.

Sports are not the only arena where this incredible focus on performance starts at a very young age. The stress of getting into an elite university can begin in ninth grade. A bad grade in algebra as a fifteen-year-old can affect a student's GPA to the point where it ruins their opportunity for acceptance to their higher education institution of choice. When I was in school, we took college placement tests once, maybe twice. There are now courses that students can take to prepare them for taking college placement tests so that they can compete with students across the country for limited spots. The competitive nature of academics has reached a new level. It can be a hard pill to swallow when our children have to accept our second or third choice in colleges when they've worked this hard for their goals and dreams.

The Price for Perfection

We have trained ourselves and our children, me included, to believe that failure is not an option. In fact, many respectable sources tell us that the way to ensure that we will reach our goals is to not even have a plan B. Plan A is the only possibility. As a culture, we have convinced ourselves that we're better than second place. We have to be the biggest, brightest, most successful, or wealthiest, or we have failed.

Don't get me wrong: I am all for aiming high. It's important not to underestimate the value in setting goals for ourselves. As we discussed in chapter 3, if we don't determine who we are and what we want to be, then someone else will. Constructing an ambitious plan, putting in the necessary time and effort to make it a reality, and never giving up are all admirable. This ambition and drive—the feeling of being imperviable to failure—are to be applauded.

But they come at a price. The price is our sense of personal peace. We lie awake at night obsessing about our failures and how we can work harder to be…well, perfect. The reason that adults and children alike are experiencing anxiety issues at unprecedented levels is because we have told ourselves that failure isn't an option. If something doesn't go according to plan, we are weak and imperfect.

Guess what…we're by default weak and imperfect. Let yourself off the hook.

Failure Is an Option

So, what if we fail? What happens when failure turns out to be a viable option? There are times when our plan of playing professional baseball, going to law school, joining the military, performing on Broadway, or being signed by a major record label doesn't materialize in the time-frame that we are convinced it would. Our window for fulfilling our dreams is closing fast, or at least we tell ourselves this. What if we are rejected by the MLB, the Screen Actors Guild, Harvard Law, etc.? Despite our best efforts, there are times when plan A becomes a tiny speck in the rear view mirror. Should we just quit or lower our expectations?

The fear of failure doesn't just apply to long-term, "dream big" goals either. This fear is constantly on our minds in our day-to-day routines. We're afraid that we won't get everything done on our to-do list today, or that the proposal we've spent the last six weeks putting together at work will be rejected, or that we will mess up the recipe that we're making for dinner tonight, or that our spouse won't like the birthday gift we bought for them, and the list goes on. Let's not forget that "trial and error" is often the most effective process for determining the best and most successful solution to any problem. We want to be perfect on the first try, but that's just not realistic or productive.

Think about it this way: let's say that you have vacation plans in Florida with your family. You've planned for three months for this trip, and the car is now loaded and everyone is ready for a road trip. The first ten hours of the journey go by without incident, but as you are heading south on I-95 through Georgia, there's a flashing sign saying, "Road Closed Ahead." Flooding has caused a road closure on your current route. What do you do now? Do you turn around and go back home?

Of course not. You find a detour to get around the roadblock so that you can continue toward your destination.

No Is Just for Now

Failure can actually be a springboard to success, taking us places that we would not typically go if we had never encountered obstacles. It causes us to work harder, dream bigger, and think outside of the proverbial box. It appears that there is a certain level of success that can only be accessed by the will, opportunities, and grit that come as a direct result from failure and setbacks. G. K. Chesterton, a theologian from the early twentieth century said this: "One sees great things from the valley; only small things from the peak."[47]

Personally, I've observed that there are very few pathways to success that do not originate, or at the very least travel through, the valley of rejection and trials.

Success is a funny thing. It can't be predicted with a formula; intelligence, skill, and opportunity do not guarantee achievement. When success comes too quickly and too easily, it's very hard to sustain.

You are probably familiar with NLF elites Tom

Brady, Shannon Sharp, and Antonio Brown. But are you familiar with the names Aaron Maybin, Russell Erxleben, David Klingler, Andre Wadsworth, Courtney Brown, Cedric Benson, Trev Alberts, Curtis Enis, Tony Mandarich, Ryan Leaf, or JaMarcus Russell? Even if they sound remotely familiar, they are certainly not household names. You may be surprised to find that they were all NFL first-round draft picks.[48]

Yes, they were the top of their class, the cream of the crop. They were told that they couldn't fail. They were courted by the top agents in the country and were probably voted "Most Likely to Succeed" by their high school classmates. But all of their talent and good fortune couldn't guarantee a contract with the NFL.

Walt Disney said, "I think it's important to have a good hard failure when you're young…because it makes you kind of aware of what can happen to you. Because of it I've never had any fear in my whole life when we've been near collapse and all of that. I've never been afraid."[49]

Below are some names you may be familiar with. These men and women all experienced some good, hard failure when they were young that provided the springboard for their success:

- Steven Spielberg, famed film producer whose movies have grossed more than $9 billion and won three Academy Awards, was rejected twice by Southern California's School of the Arts.
- Jerry Seinfeld was booed off the stage at his first show.
- Michael Jordan was cut from his high school basketball team.
- Elvis Presley was told that he couldn't sing.
- Bill Gates's first business failed.
- Katy Perry was dropped by three record labels by the age of twenty-four.

- Charles Shultz's cartoons were rejected by his high school yearbook staff.
- Madonna was fired from Dunkin Donuts after accidently squirting jelly on a customer (ha ha, that's great).
- Jay-Z was turned down by every major record label, so he started selling CDs out of the trunk of his car in order to make ends meet. He later started his own recording label.
- Sylvester Stallone was rejected 1,500 times by talent scouts and agents. He was offered $325,000 for his Rocky script on the condition that he would not star in the film. Eventually he accepted just $35,000 and a percentage of the film's sales so that he could play the lead role. The movie grossed over $200 million at the box office![50]

Failure is inevitable, but quitting should not be an option.

We have the choice to assign value to our failure, or just wear the big L on our forehead and give up and go home. We always have a choice. A wise woman once told me, "If plan A doesn't work, the alphabet has 25 more letters—204 if you're in Japan." [51]

It's Not How You Start but How You Finish

I mentioned Tom Brady earlier. Did you realize that, unlike the men mentioned above who were first-round draft picks, Brady was drafted number 199 in the 2000 NFL draft? I would imagine that people attending the event were ready to pack up and go home by the time his name was called. I was amazed to discover that Brady, the only NFL player to be honored with four Super Bowl MVP awards, was not good enough in ninth grade to start the season on the 0–8 JV team that had not scored a touchdown all year.[52]

Also joining the group of late-to-the-party, low draft picks who experience breakout success in the NFL is the highest paid player in NFL history, Kirk Cousins (fourth round), along with Terrell Davis (sixth round), Antonio Brown (sixth round), Shannon Sharpe (seventh round), Richard Sherman (fifth round), and Johnny Unitas (ninth round). It's interesting to note that Unitas, a football legend in the 1950s, was cut from the Pittsburgh Steelers and forced to take a job in construction before winning a tryout with the Indianapolis Colts.[53]

There are times when conditions outside of our control steal our plan A, right out from underneath us. Several years back there was a contestant on the popular reality show *America's Got Talent* by the name of Mandy Harvey. Mandy was pursuing a degree in Music Education at a local university when she lost her hearing from a connective tissue disorder.[54] What started as a cold developed into a virus that damaged her hearing permanently. She recalled the worst day of her life: She was sitting in class waiting for the music to start so that she and her classmates could chart the notes for an exam. As she was still waiting for the music to begin, one by one the rest of her classmates put down their pencils and exited the room. Her hearing was so damaged that she didn't know that the music was playing. She was devastated. That was the day she realized that her dream of a career in music education was gone forever.

Then, nearly ten years later, she stood on the stage waiting to be judged for the performance of her original song. Even though she still couldn't hear the music, she didn't allow it to stop her from pursuing her passion. To compensate, she took off her shoes so that she could feel the floor's vibrations for her cue to come in. Was that her original plan? Of course not, but Mandy didn't quit. Yes, it took her some time to regroup, but she didn't pack up her toys and go home, even when the situation looked bleak.

Re-purpose Rejection

Rejection is similar to that detour on the way to your vacation home. Like detours, these setbacks can throw a wrench in our plans and waste valuable time, leaving us miserable and frustrated. *But rejection, like a detour, is a necessary evil.* Detours steer us away from danger in order to get us back on track for reaching our destination. Rejection can also guide us away from traps that could shipwreck our chances for success.

It reminds me of a story that my father used to tell:

A battleship had been at sea on its routine maneuvers under heavy weather for days. The captain, who was worried about the deteriorating weather conditions, stayed on the bridge to keep an eye on all activities.

One night, the lookout on the bridge suddenly shouted, "Captain! A light, bearing on the starboard bow."

"Is it stationary or moving astern?" the captain asked.

The lookout replied that it was stationary. This meant the battleship was on a dangerous collision course with the other ship. The captain immediately ordered his signalman to signal to the ship: "We are on a collision course. I advise you to change course 20 degrees east."

Back came a response from the other ship: "You change course 20 degrees west."

Agitated by the arrogance of the response, the captain asked his signalman to shoot out another message: "I am a captain, you change course 20 degrees east."

Back came the second response: "I am a second-class seaman, you had still better change course 20 degrees west."

The captain was furious! He shouted to the signalman to send back a final message: "I am a battleship. Change course 20 degrees east right now."

Back came the flashing response: "I am a lighthouse."

The captain changed his course 20 degrees west.[55]

In the same way, failure can redirect us. It took me a long time to recognize that failure and rejection were not signs to give up; they were an indication that I needed to change my course twenty degrees! Being rejected by a prospective employer or publishing company didn't mean that I should quit looking for a job or trying to get my book published. It wasn't a sign that I was a failure and should just give up. It meant that I needed to switch gears and try another company or contact.

Rejection was an indication that the employer or the publishing house I was pursuing wasn't the best fit for me at that time. Being offered the wrong position, even with the right company, could cause a setback that would take me years to overcome. I trusted that even when I couldn't see more than two steps in front of my face, I needed to keep doing what I knew to do.[56]

I have understood for a long time that God has a plan and purpose for my life, but what I have recently come to appreciate is that failure—missteps, rejection, and disappointments—is an important part of His plan for me. My failures, more than my successes, have shaped who I am and presented a path forward. Failure creates the type of resiliency that we've discussed in previous chapters.

The Wrap-Up

For the sake of our sanity we need to realize that failure is not only an option, but an inevitable reality. Resist the need to be perfect 100 percent of the time. The question is not, *Am I going to fail?* The question is, *What will I do with my failure?* If we choose to learn from our mistakes and shortcomings, we will have the opportunity to reach new heights that we could not otherwise achieve.

Our frustration comes, not because we can't have it all, but because we can't have it all right now. Moving on to plan B is not the same as failing. Plan B is often the new, improved version of plan A. Sometimes, when we are willing to abandon what we have believed all of our life to be plan A—the individual we thought we would marry, the career we thought we would have, the role we thought we would play—we are conceding that God had something much greater planned for us that our finite minds could simply not comprehend. In the words of Thomas Rhett, "We make our plans and we hear God laughing."[57] Sometimes we need to thank God for unanswered prayers.

Even when we fail morally and suffer dire consequences for our choices God is not so small-mindedthat he can't redeem our mistakes and chart a new course for us. After all, He is the author of "Plan B." The Creator of the universe gave man free will to make his own choices. We understand when we read the account of Noah's ark and the flood that when God created mankind, *failure was an option.* We are not perfect, nor can we be. He understands our propensity toward self-destruction and still doesn't give up on us.

The only marks for failure that show up in the scorebook are when we quit or don't try at all. When we experience failure and rejection, we should recognize that we aren't perfect. Like God's plan for us, our plan for ourselves should be dynamic—marked by usually continuous and productive activity or change.[58] Plan B isn't failure, it's progress.

Buckle Up

The Key to Overcoming Irrational Fear

The older my father got, the more he enjoyed taking risks. He was still playing competitive softball in his late sixties until his body would no longer cooperate. I remember taking him to the emergency room when he was sixty-five, because he had ruptured his Achilles tendon during a game. But he wasn't willing to even go to the hospital until *after* his workout the next day. It was a gym day, and he didn't miss the gym for anything. We came to understand that Dad was more afraid of becoming old and sick than he was of dying. He told us that he wanted to "die with his boots on" (metaphorically, of course). His fear of slowing down as he got older drove him to do things that seemed reckless to others.

My family adopted Dad's mantra of "Live until you die." The implication was that playing it safe by not taking risks wasn't really living at all. As a result, no one in our immediate family would ever question the decision to buy a motorcycle, join the military, or travel across the world. (But yes, other people think we are crazy.) When making big life choices, or smaller, more common selections, our first question is rarely, Is it really safe? We never used this as a license to be careless, but making choices based on the lack of risk just wasn't the top consideration in the decision-making matrix. My father's fear of not-living-while-he-was-still-alive was passed on to the rest of us.

Fear isn't just limited to concern about physical harm. Some people are fearful about almost everything. We all know people who worry if they have enough money, or if someone is mad at them, or about the weather or what they should wear, and the list goes on. In fact, these people aren't happy unless they have something to worry about. On the other side, however, are those who seem to take unwarranted risks. They will pack up their belongings and move across the country without having a plan. These are the ones that are asked rhetorically, *What were you thinking?*

In the same way that guilt serves a purpose in the human experience, so does fear. Fear should cause us to assess the risks, without rendering us paralyzed by that fear. We've all heard the expression, "No risk, no reward." But not all risks are worth taking. Is there a way to tell good risks from bad ones? I think it's important to separate our fears into two categories: rational and irrational. Rational fear keeps us from doing anything stupid; irrational fear prevents us from doing anything useful. Healthy people allow fear to intervene, but not interfere.

Assessing Risk

In order to tell the difference between rational and irrational fear, we need to conduct a risk assessment. The risk matrix was first developed by NASA in 2009 and has been used extensively by various people and organizations from the Department of Defense to farmers.[59] The matrix considers both the impact (minor, moderate, significant, or severe) and the likelihood (low, medium, or high) in order to calculate a score to be used in decision-making. I found this very useful when I worked in the safety department of a construction company. Before deciding on how much time and resources we were willing to invest in a safety system or program, we would evaluate the potential consequences. For example, since the threat of being struck by lightning while on a jobsite is relatively low, it would not warrant an expensive and elaborate solution. But the threat of electrical shock from using extension cords plugged into ungrounded sources was relatively high and the solution was inexpensive; it warranted our attention. I've included an example of a risk matrix below for your reference.[60]

		Impact →			
	Negligible	Minor	Moderate	Significant	Severe
Very Likely	Low Med	Medium	Med Hi	High	High
Likely	Low	Low Med	Medium	Med Hi	High
Possible	Low	Low Med	Medium	Med Hi	Med Hi
Unlikely	Low	Low Med	Low Med	Medium	Med Hi
Very Unlikely	Low	Low	Low Med	Medium	Medium

(Likelihood axis on left, from Very Likely down to Very Unlikely)

This is an excellent tool that can be adapted to analyze complex situations in order to make a rational decision. But unless you are an engineer or a physicist, you may not need to analytically evaluate every decision to this extent in your day-to-day lives. So instead I've provided some simple questions to help us decide if our fear is rational or irrational, and the potential risks to our physical and emotional well-being. Asking these questions will help you to understand if the risk is real or perceived, how to lessen the risk, and evaluate whether the benefits could potentially outweigh the dangers.

1. Is my fear based on facts and experience or feelings and perceptions?

Sometimes there is no threat posed to our well-being at all, but because an activity is new to us it seems threatening. I would dare say that many who are afraid to fly fall into this category. Unless they have survived a plane crash, their fear is not rooted in personal experience.

I'll admit, flying commercial airlines is not my favorite thing to do. On our flight home from Uganda, we had to go through three security checkpoints while inside the airport prior to boarding a connecting flight. That's right, we never stepped outside of the terminal but still were subject to three separate security checks after a five-hour flight, and prior to boarding another one scheduled to be in the air for another fourteen hours. As annoying as it was, it alleviated any fear that our plane could be hijacked. If my bottle of water that I purchased in the terminal couldn't make it through security, I was confident that bad guys couldn't either.

I am not afraid to fly. I may not like to fly, but it's not healthy or advantageous for me to base my fears on my feeling rather than facts. The fact of the matter is that flying is the safest mode of transportation. The odds of dying in a plane crash are eleven million to one. My chance of dying in a car or traffic accident, however, is significantly greater at one in five thousand. In fact, it is more likely that I could be killed by a falling coconut than in a plane crash.[61]

The argument against the fear of flying is one of the simplest illustrations to cite, but I challenge you to ask this question in evaluating *every* fear. Some fears are very legitimate; they are based on facts and should be taken seriously. For example, you may have a fear of being electrocuted while using a hair dryer while taking a bath. That's a valid fear.

Is your fear based on legitimate facts and information, or is it more of a preference? My mother-in-law told me recently that she was allergic to dogs. I was surprised to find that out now after knowing her for over thirty years. After I inquired a little further, she revealed that she wasn't physically allergic; she didn't like them. She was mentally allergic, as she put it (ha ha). Sometimes fear is a preference made out of convenience or lack of knowledge, but it's not in response to a legitimate threat.

2. How can I mitigate the risks?

As I mentioned earlier, my husband and I don't discourage our kids from taking risks. At the same time, we don't encourage them to blindly engage in high-risk activities such as driving and hunting without requiring them to take every realistic precaution. When our son wanted a crossbow for Christmas last year, for example, we required him to take an online safety course before we would even *buy* it for him for Christmas. Yes, he needed to take that course before he could get his hunting license, but we insisted that he finish the class before he would even have the opportunity to handle the weapon.

We don't have to fear situations—even ones that carry inherent risks—but we shouldn't blindly accept any of those risks either.

3. Does the potential gain outweigh the inherent risks?

This answer to this question may seem simple and clear, but I challenge you to evaluate this constantly, as conditions can change very quickly. For example, many things we do when we're younger can carry more risk as we get older. Buying a brand-new vehicle on credit has fewer ramifications to a young working professional than a middle-aged single mom who is the primary provider for her three children. Playing in a recreational hockey league out of college is a great way to stay in shape and keep up with the guys. Playing in that same league and risking a serious injury when that guy is forty and self-employed as a contractor with no disability insurance may not be the best move.

I'm all for riding motorcycles. Yes, it's a risk, but as long as the rider takes reasonable safety measure (such as wearing a helmet, whether the law requires it or not), I don't see a problem with it...in most situations. There was a certain professional athlete in my hometown who crashed his motorcycle while riding during the season and without a helmet. Risking a multimillion-dollar contract in order as wealth, success, or power can even make us feel that we are immune to risk. We feel untouchable, which ironically makes us more vulnerable. In these situations, there may not be any gain to be had, but our internal risk assessor is broken.

Not all risks or benefits can be measured in terms of just physical safety either. Playing a sport, riding a motorcycle, traveling across the country or world can open new opportunities and contacts that we wouldn't gain otherwise. I would argue that our life's goal shouldn't be to play it safe. What fun is that? New ventures, whether they be starting a new company, enlisting in the military, having another child, or moving to a new neighborhood, can carry significant risks. But without taking those chances, we are destined to live very small, simple lives, and risk missing out on the great adventure that God has been preparing for us since we were born.

4.   What is the worst thing that can happen?

I listed this last because it is the most subjective of the questions, but typically this is the first question I ask myself. The truth of the matter is that there are a lot of things I am afraid of that are not legitimate fears. I am afraid of being rejected by a prospective employer, afraid of looking stupid in front of my co-workers, afraid that my ideas will be shot down by my boss, afraid of making my kids mad at me, afraid of appearing insignificant to those more successful than me, and the list goes on. More often than not, when I ask, *What is the worst thing that can happen?*, the answer is so petty it doesn't merit my time even considering it.

You may have heard of the now infamous research experiment first conducted in 1968 by Bibb Latane and John Darley. Unsuspecting job applicants were directed to a conference room to complete their applications. Little did they know that the other applicants in the room were paid actors. When smoke begins to infiltrate the room under the doors, the actors were instructed to ignore it and not respond. As you may predict, nine out of ten of the subjects followed the lead of the others and continued to fill out their applications. Some even rubbed their eyes and waved the smoke away from their faces, but they didn't respond to the potential threat.[62]

As wrong as it may be to view this through the lens of hindsight, it's a great example of a situation where the participants did *not* ask what is the worst thing that can happen. If they had, they may have recognized that the potential embarrassment of speaking up sure beats the alternative of being trapped in a burning building. Personally, I have discovered that asking this question helps me to filter through the long list of nonsense fears that would otherwise keep me thinking small and acting even smaller. Sometimes I'm afraid to do something that I sense I'm being prompted to do. My fear isn't valid, but still I use it as a good excuse to do nothing. For example, when we considered holding our first FUSION Leadership Conference, I had to ask myself, *What is the worst thing that could happen?* I had organized enough events to know how to plan, so I knew I could potentially lose a little bit of money but not a significant amount. I concluded that the answer to that question was that no one may sign up to attend—that would be the worst thing that could happen. Now, a year and four conferences later, I understand that the reward greatly outweighed any risk that truly existed.

Often, asking this question forces me to let go of my crutch. I use this with my family too. I've said it for so long that before they can even verbalize their fear, they say, "I know, I know…what's the worst thing that can happen, right?" Ha ha, right on.

What If?

What happens, however, if you ask this question and the answer is daunting to you? My friend shared that reading about the odds of getting into a car accident (five thousand to one) made her want to stay in the house for the rest of the day. Sometimes our fears seem rational to us, even though others may not agree. If you find that fear is a constant struggle, I challenge to really examine if your fear is truly rational, or if it could be irrational. Below are some additional questions that could help you evaluate:

Is the outcome I fear a probable reality?

We discussed the risk matrix earlier in the chapter. This formula considered both the impact and the probability. Yes, the impact of an accident could potentially be significant, but statistics don't tell the whole story. How probable is it that you will be involved in a car accident on your way to work *today*? The answer is, "not very." It's a possibility but not a probability. Think of all the people you know who drive to work every day for years and have never had an accident. If your fear, however, is that it will rain on your Memorial Day picnic, the probability rating will be much higher. But the potential impact is significantly lower than the previously mentioned event.

Is there anything I fear more?

Yes, it's a risk every time you get in your car. But remember, the purpose of fear is to make us alert. As we mentioned above, do everything you can to minimize the risks. Allow this fear to drive you to always wear your seat belt, drive defensively, and ensure that your car is properly maintained. In the final analysis, however, I find that the fear of dying of starvation motivates me to take the risk of driving to the grocery store (smile).

Is my fear nearsighted?

Sometimes we need to consider the fact that maybe we're not seeing the big picture. Our tunnel vision may be keeping us trapped in the here and now. Everything we do that is considered worthwhile carries some level of risk. If I choose to focus on my fear, I could lose out on the joy of owning a home, having a child, or finding a job that I love. Don't get caught in that trap.

Are there physiological reasons why my fear seems exacerbated?

Since our body, soul, and spirit are so closely linked, it is very possible that physical conditions are interfering with our ability to reason. Medications, an illness, or a condition could be short-circuiting your emotions. (I can tell you that my brain did not function properly when I was pregnant.) Please consult with your doctor if you suspect that a hormonal imbalance is causing your fears to escalate.

Am I afraid, or do I just want to always be in control?

Let's face it, often fear comes because we don't have control over every situation in our lives. We want to order the chaos, but we can't. The concept of Living Free requires that we control those things that we can control and let go of what we can't.

Please understand this is only a high-level overview and there is so much more we could say on this subject. Don't hesitate to seek professional help if fear is getting the best of you.

The Wrap-Up

Remember, as we have discussed in earlier chapters, your mind is your battlespace and the struggle is real. Fear can render us hopeless and helpless if we don't take control of our minds. If we truly want to Live Free and not be trapped in the small thinking that can hold us back from doing anything worthwhile, we need to evaluate every fear by conducting a risk assessment. A risk matrix can be used for more complex problem solving, but often, asking yourself a few simple questions will do the trick.

1. Is my fear based on facts and experience or feelings and perceptions?
2. How can I mitigate the risks?
3. Does the potential gain outweigh the inherent risks?
4. What is the worst thing that can happen?

After conducting your own risk assessment, you should know if the threat is real or perceived. If the threat is real, does the perspective benefit outweigh the risk? If after conducting an assessment you determine that it does, then buckle up and enjoy the ride!

10

Look through the Turn

The Key to Being Kind, Not Just Acting Like It

It's a long-standing joke in my family that my marriage to Perry was arranged by my parents. That's not exactly how it happened, but it isn't entirely untrue either. No, my father did not pay a dowry to his family. It wasn't *that* kind of arranged marriage. But my parents did spot him first and bring him home, so to speak. Dad was the coach of the church softball team and Perry played for the team. Those two were good friends before I came into the picture. My mom, however, made sure I came into the picture. Anytime I was at one of their games, Mom would whisper, "Go talk to Perry!" I was still in high school at the time and he was a few years older, so this went on for a year or two until I graduated. That summer, however, we finally caught each other's attention. Perry's side of the story is that he asked the coach's daughter out to secure a spot on the team.

My parents saw traits in Perry that they would want for their daughter's spouse. He was kind, hardworking, and respectful to his mom and women in general. All I saw was that he was really good-looking—blonde hair, green eyes, athletic build. And he had a motorcycle! That sealed the deal for me.

Now, thirty years later, I am beyond grateful that Mom and Dad were looking a little beyond the surface. In fact, they did such a stellar job picking my husband that Perry and I tried to arrange our children's marriages too. As you may imagine, that didn't fly.

There was a study done in the 1970s by psychologist John Gottman to uncover the secrets that make or break a marriage relationship. He and his colleague Robert Levenson gathered newlywed couples at their laboratory, called "The Love Lab," and hooked them up to electrodes.[63] The couples then answered questions about their relationship, including how they met, any major conflicts, and positive memories. Readings were taken on whether an individual was calm and relaxed or showed the "fight or flight" response, even to simple questions.

The couples were then observed over the next six years. According to their results, the researchers separated the couples into two groups: the masters and the disasters. The masters tended to be respectful of and grateful toward their partners. The disasters, on the other hand, were only focused on their partner's mistakes and were very critical.

The most critical finding in this entire study is that there is one particular trait that correlated to lasting, stable relationships: *kindness*. Kindness is like a language of its own that can break through any barrier. It's the glue that binds together every relationship, not just marriages. This got me thinking how we can increase the kindness factor in our lives in order to have healthy, long-lasting relationship in our families, our workplaces, and communities. After considerable thought, the conclusion I reached is that the first step is to recognize what it means to be kind, not just act it.

Just like everything else in our culture, we've made kindness performance based. There's a lot of talk about *acts* of kindness. If someone gets "caught" buying diapers for a single mom or helping an old lady cross the street or giving money to a homeless man, they become instant celebrities on social media. In fact, people video themselves helping someone less fortunate so that they can post it on Facebook. (I find it interesting how even acts of kindness can become self-serving.) It's important to acknowledge that there's difference between acting kind and being kind. Acts of kindness are fantastic and make us feel warm and fuzzy inside. The problem is that they can make us appear kind, but they don't make us kind.

And here's why: kindness is an output, not an input.[64]

Kindness isn't meant to be an act; it should be part of our character. Our actions flow out from our thoughts and feelings. Our actions don't typically change how we think and feel, at least not permanently. If they did, we wouldn't constantly struggle to be in shape, quit drinking, or get over a broken relationship. One workout, one day sober, or one blind date and we would be cured. Likewise, one act of kindness would make us kind to our spouses, children, or co-workers all the time. But our mind, will, and emotions direct our actions, not the other way around. Our hearts act as our personal GPS unit directing us where to go, how to act, and what to say. Using the GPS illustration, our words and actions give away our location.

Let me give you an illustration. I heard a story recently about a very successful business man who donated $2 million to construct a new cancer treatment wing for a local hospital. This was a very commendable act, so there was a big write-up in the paper about him, and he was honored at a fancy gala event. What the article didn't mention is that this man hadn't spoken to either of his two adult children in several years, and how he managed to get out of his end of any agreement he made with his ex-wife during the divorce settlement. His co-workers characterized him as mean and cold hearted. The sum of our actions, not a single act, gives away our location.

Three Keys to Being Kind

In order to *be* kind, we have to deal with the underlying issues that can make us unkind, and downright mean sometimes. I want to share with you three ways to change your thinking in order to increase the kindness factor in your life:

1. Forgive easily.

We live in a culture that teaches us that we have rights: we have the right to be happy, we have the right to be respected, we have the right to be treated like everyone else. That's all well and good…as long as people actually treat us well. But if not, it causes us a lot of anxiety. All of this emotional entitlement is exhausting, because it requires us to hold on to all the unpaid invoices, if you will. This is one of the many ways that we are encouraged to be selfish in our culture, because it's all about *me*.

> *I can't believe you did that to me.*
> *You can't treat me that way.*
> *What about me?*

We lay awake at night thinking about what so-and-so did or didn't do. Holding on to all those debts that will never come due—real or perceived—makes us not only tired, but unhappy, unfulfilled, and, frankly, unkind.

I can hear the objections now, *But he needs to pay, or she needs to pay for this.* Rest assured that there are always consequences to our actions—both good and bad. And just because consequences don't happen on our timetable doesn't because consequences don't happen on our timetable doesn't mean that they're not coming. A friend explained it to me this way a long time ago: just because we let someone off of our hook, doesn't mean that God lets them off of His. I find that oddly reassuring.

So, the next time your spouse, a friend, or a random stranger offends you, give them a pass. Remember the game Monopoly? Instead of a "Get Out of Jail Free" card, consider it an "Act Like a Jerk" card. Just let it go. We are not talking about allowing someone to walk all over us like a door mat. That doesn't benefit anyone. We're talking about making a conscious decision to not allow someone else's choices that you have no control over to ruin *your* day. I've heard it explained this way: holding on to resentment (and unforgiveness) "is like letting someone you despise live rent-free in your head."[65]

And yes, you might give out enough free passes to certain individuals that they might be able to ride all day at Kennywood Park, but it's ok. You will sleep better. That alone will make us kinder.

2. **Realize there's enough to go around.**

I have recently come to recognize that often when I have experienced conflict in my personal relationships, it is because I had a different agenda for them, or they had a different agenda for me than the one that we had for ourselves. Sometimes it's easy to see the connection. For example, my agenda for my husband on a Sunday afternoon could be for him to take out trash and mow the lawn, but his agenda for himself is to lie on the couch and watch football all day.

Oftentimes, though, our agendas are hidden—even to us. My subliminal agenda, for example, could be for you to be less successful, less attractive, less kind because somehow in my mind that makes me feel better about myself. Maybe my agenda is for you to hold the same beliefs that I do because Oftentimes, though, our agendas are hidden—even to us. My subliminal agenda, for example, could be for you to be less successful, less attractive, less kind because somehow in my mind that makes me feel better about myself. Maybe my agenda is for you to hold the same beliefs that I do because somehow it diminishes my views when you think differently from me. The problem is that whether we realize it or not, we tend to view success as a commodity. We're concerned that there is only so much of it to go around.[66] When someone else gets a promotion over us, or buys a brand-new car that we can't afford, or has something else that we can't have, it's as if they are taking a piece of the pie, our pie, which leaves less for us. Often, it's hard for us to be kind if we fear that the other person is getting ahead…and taking all of our pie!

The truth is, there is more than enough to go around. Your happiness, success, and fulfillment in no way detracts from my happiness, success, or fulfillment. Even if you receive the promotion that I wanted, I need to be mature enough to recognize that it's not my last chance to be promoted or to find a job a job that I love. It's easy to get caught up in the game of trying to measure up, but it's not productive.

3.   Don't engage.

Are you familiar with the phrase *rules of engagement*? This is a military term referring to the circumstances under which it is not advised to engage with the enemy in a combat situation. It's my personal observation that there are social rules of engagement too, and they are different for men and women. For example, a man is very hesitant to say anything about another man that may be construed as disrespect. It's "man code," which I'm told is a real thing. Sometimes this is very helpful in maintaining relationships, but at the same time it could prevent him from speaking up in a meeting to challenge his boss's idea, even if he disagrees. But this same man can be lured out to the parking lot to settle a dispute, if challenged to do so.

Women, however, would rather talk things out than

engage physically (most women, anyway). We have an easier time discussing our feelings and voicing our opinion. There are down sides to the "woman code" rules of engagement, as well. If you ask women which demographic they would rather work with, 90 percent will respond that they prefer working with men. Why? Because all that discussion about feelings and opinions can seem caddy. Translated, this means that women just naturally create more drama than men.

A paradigm shift came for me personally when I realized that I don't have to engage in the drama, even when it's directed at me. I always have a choice to respond with kindness, rather than to react out of anger or frustration.

There was a situation that occurred not too long ago. I was working on a big project and a week before the deadline, one individual backed out on her commitment. She sent a long email about why she made this decision and it was really my fault, because I didn't uphold my end of the deal. That wasn't even true! I actually had our agreement in writing and a time-stamped email where I spelled out my intentions, and she signed off on the plan.

At that point I had a choice. I had to evaluate the situation and see if this was one of those times where I needed to push through and hold her "feet to the fire," but it wasn't. It was a done deal and there's nothing I could have done—except cause a lot of drama. I could have hit Reply All and explained my position and how I had evidence that she wasn't being honest, and that she was the one not upholding her end of the deal.

Regardless, it's my choice whether I engage or not. To be honest, I was more than a little frustrated and tempted to strike back. But I have come to realize that most people fall into one of two categories: 1) they already know what's really going on (i.e., the character of both parties), or 2) they simply don't care. In this instance, I chose to reply back (just to her) and say, "I understand. I'll pursue other options. Thanks for the response."

The remarkable thing was that plan B was a hundred times better than plan A. The other remarkable thing is how much lower my anxiety level is when I willfully give up my right to defend my point of view.

Kindness Is a Discipline

About fifteen years ago, I had the opportunity to take the motorcycle safety course and get my class M license. My husband found a little older-model 200cc Honda for me. It was kind of a joke of a motorcycle, but it got me from place A to place B, except for when it didn't. The most challenging part for me of learning to ride is what the instructors refer to as "looking through the turn." This means that you keep your head up and your eyes looking where you want to go. It sounds intuitive, but it's not. It's much easier and feels more natural to look down and see where you are currently. The problem is that this makes it difficult to maneuver the bike through a turn because it's easy to misjudge the depth of the corner.

In the same way, kindness requires us to keep our head up and look beyond a lot of junk that is happening at ground level. This is the trouble with being kind rather than simply acting: it's not as much fun. For example, when you hand a random stranger a bottle of water on a hot day, they thank you for your kindness. When you announce that you have donated money to a charity, they send a thank-you note or recognize you publicly. When you help an older lady across the street, someone may actually be recording you on their smartphone. They could post it on Facebook and your act of random kindness could get two thousand likes. We may not think of it in this way, but sometimes public acts of kindness are often a cry for attention. If our focus is really on helping other then we're not looking for recognition.

On the other hand, no one is going to say, *Thank you for not blasting your boss's mistake in a Reply All email to the whole company,* or *Thank you for not broadcasting your spouse's indiscretion throughout the neighborhood,* or *Thank you for not allowing the comment that your mother made to you about your children cause a family feud that lasts until your now-two-year-old graduates from high school.* No one will thank you for looking through the turn *because no one knows what you know.* There is no one else to share in the gossip. Well, that's not fun. No, it's not, but that's the nature of being kind and not just acting it out when others are looking.

It's important to stop for a second and recognize that we're not talking about interfering with the natural consequences of someone else's choices. An example would be hiding evidence or withholding details about a friend's actions that may get them in trouble with the law. That's actually not kind, because it enables self-destructive behavior. I'm talking about your response and my response when someone doesn't treat us how we deserve to be treated.

The Wrap-Up

Kindness is the X factor in most every human relationship, from marriage to friendship to work. Increasing our ability to be kind will help foster healthy relationships in every aspect of our lives. Being kind is much more than just committing random acts of kindness. We have the ability to choose how to respond, even in difficult situations where we are mistreated or disrespected. The sum of our words and actions—not just those performed for an audience—act as a GPS unit giving away our heart's location.

Often kindness is more about what we let go than what we give. We can choose to look through the turn, to keep our heads up and look beyond the ugliness. But the amazing thing is, even when we let go of offenses committed against us, God knows. He's the only one who can vindicate us and give us favor…even with those who are difficult to please.

Avoid the Crowds

The Key to Being Free

One of my favorite memories from when I was younger was our tradition for the day after Thanksgiving. My mom, aunt Nancy, and cousin Dana would take the bus to town for a day of shopping and lunch. (Yes, this was Black Friday, but I don't think it was known as that at that time.) We would walk past the department store window displays that were decorated for Christmas. There was one last stop we made before boarding the bus for home—the candy store! This was my favorite part of the day. Sadly, some things have not changed.

Even as we got older and had our own children, we kept the tradition going for a while. We no longer took a bus downtown, but all the ladies in the family would meet up for a day of food and shopping. But as the trend toward on-line shopping has skyrocketed, sometimes my mom and I opt to just meet for coffee and shop on Amazon in order to avoid the crowds.

The older I get, the more I have come to realize that the key to Living Free is to avoid the crowds. No, I'm not talking about staying away from the shopping malls during the holiday season. I'm talking about the same thing that we have discussed through this book: becoming an independent contractor and thinking for yourself.

Don't Do It

Just because everyone is doing it doesn't mean it's what's best for you. Each generation is convinced that they have found that hidden truth that their parent's generation was searching for, only to discover that one fad gives way to another. You are an independent contractor. Don't do anything just so you can fit in. The crowd isn't your friend. The crowd will turn on you faster than you can blink. (Who is the crowd, anyway?)

In 2017, CBS launched a new drama series entitled *Wisdom of the Crowd.*[67] The show is based on a tech innovator's attempt to create a digital platform for the general public around the world to share and review tips and evidence for criminal investigations. The driving force behind this is the main character's need to find his daughter's killer. The show was cancelled after thirteen episodes. Hmm... I don't know exactly why the show was scratched, but could it be because *there is no wisdom in the crowd*?

Group demonstrations have become very popular in recent years. Some of them have attracted thousands of people who wanted "their voice to be heard." But whose voice? Some minority groups have actually started to boycott these groups claiming to speak for minorities because, ironically, they feel they are being discriminated against. Many of us are beginning to realize that it is impossible for *my* voice to be heard in a group. As we discussed in chapter 3, the idea that the group has the right to make decisions for the individual has provided the perfect cover throughout history for the strong to exploit the weak. Avoid the crowds!

Following the crowd, or even thinking like the crowd, will rarely benefit anyone… especially you as an individual.

Avoiding the crowd and thinking for yourself means that you are the expert in your own life. You can make any decision you choose: you can marry who you want, dress how you want, pursue the career you want…but choose wisely! As we discussed in chapter 2, some of our choices will support our personal freedom, while others have the potential to imprison us—not only physically, but emotionally, socially, or spiritually. It's important to understand that we have complete control over our actions, but not over the consequences of those actions.

As we discussed in chapter 9, healthy individuals conduct a personal risk assessment to thoroughly understand the potential effects before moving forward—the good, the bad, and the ugly. Ursula Burns, the former CEO of Xerox, was the first African American woman to become CEO of a Fortune 500 company, according to Forbes Magazine.[68] She grew up in a very poor part of Lower East Manhattan, and her mother struggled to pay for her private schooling. When she excelled at math, her guidance counselor encouraged her to pursue a degree in mechanical engineering. She admits that she was one of very few women, and the only black woman, in her profession, but she viewed it as an opportunity rather than a detriment.[69]

In speaking about women in STEM careers, she said, "All of us are pioneers. A lot of what pioneers do, they do not benefit from themselves." [70] Ursula wasn't afraid to stand out from the crowd, even after conducting her own risk analysis. She understood that career advancement would be an uphill battle for her but recognized that she had a unique opportunity to roll out the red carpet for others coming behind. So she took the chance anyway.

Breaking the Cycle

Hiding in the crowd can be an easy way to avoid personal responsibility. Our culture has deceived us into thinking that we're all victims. Even when I haven't been directly targeted, if a crime has been committed against a single member of my group, the crime has—by proxy—been committed against me. If I am a victim by association, then I can claim plausible deniability for any consequence that I have brought upon myself.

To give a personal example, there was a two-year period in my life during which I was turned down for four different positions at four different companies. The interview process for each of these positions lasted anywhere from two to six months. In every one of these situations, I made it to the final round of interviews out of many, sometimes hundreds of applicants, but always came in second place. Each time the selected candidate was a man. It would have been easy for me to think that I was rejected because of being a woman, not because my skill sets or experience didn't match up to my competitors. And even if this was true—even if I was truly discriminated against because I was a female—it wasn't productive for me to claim the victim participation trophy. That trophy or title wasn't going to pay the bills or be a resume builder. Instead, I chose to use this rejection as an indication that I needed to change my course twenty degrees and pursue different avenues.

The term *groupthink* was first defined in 1952 by Merriam-Webster as "a pattern of thought characterized by self-deception, forced manufacture of consent, and conformity to group values and ethics."[71] Groupthink is in direct opposition to the idea of Living Free because it forces me, as an individual, to hold on to unpaid invoices from years, even decades, that will never become due (**see chapter** 4). This would be the equivalent of suing a company for not paying their bill when they have never used my services.

That's pure craziness. But if we going to be free, we have to avoid group-think and the victim mentality.

Sexism, racism, or any other forms of discrimination will never be solved by identifying with the crowd. When a single member of the crowd behaves badly, the entire population is labeled. "American's are rude," for example, doesn't mean that every single American acts rudely when visiting oversees, but it does apply that Americans have the reputation for being rude. Can that reputation ever change? A single documented episode of an American behaving in an unbecoming manner makes the possibility more remote. This would appear to be an uphill battle that would be impossible to win.

It's my personal observation that conflict of any kind can only be resolved the old-fashioned way: face-to-face, one-on-one. Having a "national conversation," as I hear many commentators call for, will never resolve the issue. One side will never be persuaded by the other that they were wrong, and that they should abandon their position. The more that we speak *at* each other, the further apart the chasm grows. If you doubt this, just start engaging in political discussions publicly on social media and see if you are able to convince your friends that their viewpoints are wrong.

Instead, trying meeting with one individual with whom you disagree with over coffee, and just listen for starters. My grandfather Angelo used to say, "Always listen to others, because then you will be twice as smart as them. You'll know what you know, and you'll know what they know."

You are the only one that can break the cycle of discrimination—both as the victim and/or the perpetrator—in your own life. This doesn't mean that you have not experienced prejudice or been discriminated against. Every day there are terrible crimes committed against individuals and entire races, both in our country, and around the world. The reality, however, is that whatever happens to others, or by others, is outside our direct circle of control. We can only focus on our own experience. As we discussed in chapter 5, the pain is real, but we do not need to allow it to define us.

I recently heard a story about a man by the name of Brandon Straka. Straka was raised in a small town in Nebraska where he faced discrimination, and even violence, for being gay. He made the move to New York, where he felt he would be more accepted, in order to pursue a career in acting. Things didn't go as he anticipated, however, and he felt lonelier and more isolated than ever before. This situation was exacerbated by the fact that he was unable to find meaningful work, and Brandon soon found himself steeped in alcohol and cocaine abuse.

After a couple years of this self-loathing condition, he recognized that he was the only one who had the power to change his situation. "There really is no such thing as victimhood unless you choose to be a victim," contends Straka.[72] Although it was a hard road, he got sober and has stayed that way since early 2015. Way to go, Brandon.

It's a Two-Way Street

Likewise, you are the only one who can reach outside of your comfort zone to those who do not look, think, or act in the same ways you do. You don't have to stand behind the official position of any group. Conduct your own research and build relationships with those who can challenge your thinking. Uncover the truth for yourself. You have the ability to extend kindness (true kindness, not just acts) even to those who are unkind to you. There is no guarantee that your efforts will be accepted, but we are not responsible for how our actions are perceived, only how they are intended.

The Truth Will Set You Free

Do you want to be free? Avoid the crowds and follow the God who created you and has a purpose and plan for your life.[73] He has given you a sound mind in order to achieve that purpose. God has provided detailed instructions for *you* on life, love, and how to reach your final destination in His divinely inspired and preserved memoir (i.e., the Bible).

Please understand: Religion is not the answer. Jesus is the answer. A lot of well-meaning groups (crowds) have developed elaborate systems of rules and regulations that can often become a hindrance to finding the truth about God. Religion creates an us versus them mentality, but God does not. He extends His grace and offer of salvation to all of us individually, regardless of the crowd with which we associate.

Do you want to be truly free? Then you must search for *the* truth, not whichever version is trending this month. The purpose of this chapter isn't to spell out what's true and what's not; it's to encourage you to search for it. You will only discover the truth if you are conscientiously looking for it.[74]

And That's a Wrap

You are an independent contractor who has every right and responsibility to take full control of your circumstances. Your mind is your battlespace—protect it! Fear, guilt, and other emotions serve a purpose in the human experience, but we don't have to allow them to overwhelm us and steal our joy. Learn what truly makes you happy and resist the temptation to chase after those things that your friends, social media, or Hollywood say will make you happy. Avoid the crowds and seek the truth. Learn how to be kind, not just act it.

Learning resilience and teaching it to our children is one of the best safeguards we have against anxiety and depression. But even when we experience failure because of our own actions, or tragedy as the result of circumstances beyond our control, we don't have to stay stuck in sadness, despair, or regret.

We can visit, but we don't have to live there.

Acknowledgments

The concepts in this book developed over many years, long before they were ever written on paper. I would like to thank the following people for making this vision a reality:

- My husband, Perry, for being the most patient and kind man I've ever known
- My mom, Connie Geier, and daughter, Valerie Donnelly, who entertain my crazy ideas but—at the same time—keep me from going over the edge
- Tammy Summers, for your help with proofreading, and just being the amazingly resilient woman that you are
- My friends Jenn, Maggie, and Melissa for your help proofreading and providing valuable insights
- My friends, Kathy Seitz and Linda Wilson, for sharing your wisdom
- Pastor Mark Lutz, who recognized that I was a content creator before I knew that was "a thing"
- Susan Harrer, for all of your guidance. This project would look very differently without you. Who knew what God had planned when we met at a coach's clinic fifteen years ago?
- My editor, Christy Callahan, for all of your help with smoothing the edges
- My professors at Liberty University who helped shape my thinking…twenty years after I thought I already knew it all

Notes

1 NIMH, "Any Anxiety Disorder" (2017), https://www.nimh.nih.gov/health/statistics/any-anxiety-disorder.shtml#part_155094.

2 Kristen Proby, Easy Love (Chicago: Ampersand Publishing, 2015).

3 2 Timothy 1:7.

4 NIMH, "Any Anxiety Disorder."

5 See "The Abundance Principle" in Stephen Covey, The 7 Habits of Highly Effective People. (Free Press, 1989).

6 Ryan Holiday, "7 People Who Overcame Huge Obstacles to Become Famous," Cracked.com, May 6, 2014, http://www.cracked.com/blog/7-people-who-overcame-huge-obstacles-to-become-famous/.

7 "A Quote by Ann Landers," Goodreads.com, https://www.goodreads.com/quotes/273322-hanging-onto-resentment-is-letting-someone-you-despise-live-rent-free.

8 "Battlespace Awareness Definition (US DoD)," Militaryfactory.com, 2011, https://www.militaryfactory.com/dictionary/military-terms-defined.asp?term_id=698.

9 Proverbs 4:23; Luke 6:45; 2 Corinthians 10:3–5; Philippians 4:6–7; 1 Peter 1:13; Mark 7:20–22; Romans 12:2; Colossians 3:2.

10 "7 People Who Overcame Huge Obstacles to Become Famous," Cracked.com.

11 Nora Battelle, "These Three Things Are Keeping Your Child Up at Night," Thriveglobal.com, 2018, https://www.thriveglobal.com/stories/these-three-things-are-keeping-your-child-up-at-night/.

12 H. Shaban, "Study Links Restricting Screen Time for Kids to Higher Mental Performance," Washingtonpost.com, September 27, 2018, https://www.washingtonpost.com/technology/2018/09/27/study-links-restricting-screen-time-kids-higher-mental-performance/?utm_term=.a4844b4954d9.

13 Romans 12:2.

14 "Creativity and Lifelong Learning," American Society on Aging, 2018, http://asaging.org/education-topic/creativity-and-lifelong-learning.

15 1 Corinthians 6:19–20.

16 Luke 4:42–43.

17 Reinhold Niebuhr, "Serenity Prayer," 1951, https://www.allaboutprayer.org/serenity-prayer.htm.

18 Micah 6:8.

19 John Florio and Ouisie Shapiro, "The Dark Side of Going for Gold," The Atlantic, August 18, 2016, https://www.theatlantic.com/health/archive/2016/08/post-olympic-depression/496244/.

20 "Anxiety Disorder Statistics," 2018, https://www.anxietycentre.com/anxiety-statistics-information.shtml.

21 Philip Brickman, Dan Coates, and Ronnie Janoff-Bulman, "Lottery Winners and Accident Victims: Is Happiness Relative?," Journal of Personality and Social Psychology 36, no. 8 (1978): 917–927.

22 Tim Clinton and Gary Sibcy, "Loving Your Child Too Much: How to Keep a Close Relationship with Your Child without Overindulging, Overprotecting, or Overcontrolling," (Nashville, TN: Thomas Nelson, 2006).

23 Philippians 4:12–13.

24 Jeff Haden, The Motivation Myth (Penguin Random House, 2018), 35.

25 David Chiu, "Jonestown: 13 Things You Should Know about Cult Massacre," RollingStone.com, November 17, 2017, https://www.rollingstone.com/culture/culture-features/jonestown-14-things-you-should-know-about-cult-massacre-121974/.

26 "Written Testimony of Kathi A. Aultman, MD," Judiciary.senate.gov, March 15, 2016, , https://www.judiciary.senate.gov/imo/media/doc/03-15-16%20Aultman%20Testimony.pdf.

27 Romans 2:15.

28 "The 5 Stages of Grief & Loss," Psych Central, October 8, 2018, https://psychcentral.com/lib/the-5-stages-of-loss-and-grief/.

Notes (Continued)

29 Richard Dawkins, "There's No Such Thing as Free Will," Richard Dawkins Foundation, Richarddawkins.net, May 17, 2016, https://www.richarddawkins.net/2016/05/theres-no-such-thing-as-free-will/.

30 Eric Scottberg, "9 Famous People Who Will Inspire You to Never Give Up," Themuse.com, https://www.themuse.com/advice/9-famous-people-who-will-inspire-you-to-never-give-up.

31 Renee Jacques, "16 Wildly Successful People Who Overcame Huge Obstacles to Get There," Huffpost UK, December 6, 2017, https://www.huffingtonpost.com/2013/09/25/successful-people-obstacles_n_3964459.html.

32 Psalm 34:18.

33 Psalm 68:5.

34 Isaiah 41:10.

35 Philippians 4:13.

36 Philippians 4:9.

37 Jeremiah 29:11.

38 "Monitoring Your Child | SCAN," Scanva.org, https://www.scanva.org/support-for-parents/parent-resource-center-2/monitoring-your-child/.

39 Mark Obmascik, Kevin Simpson, and Stacie Oulton, "Columbine: Parents Blindsided by Plot," DenverPost.com, Nov. 22, 2000, http://extras.denverpost.com/news/col1122.htm.

40 David Code, To Raise Happy Kids, Put Your Marriage First (Chicago: The Crossroad Publishing Company, 2014).

41 "Raising Resilient Kids," ICAN, January 24, 2017, http://icanaz.org/raising-resilient-kids.

42 CBS News, "Junkyard or Playground Paradise? Kids Making Their Own Adventures," 2016, TV program.

43 Ibid.

44 CBS News, "Americans to Receive Cellphone Alert from Trump in First National Test," Cbsnews.com, October 3, 2018, https://www.cbsnews.com/news/presidential-alert-test-fema-national-crises/.

45 Romans 12:18; Hebrews 12:14

46 Michael Olpin and Margie Hesson, Stress Management for Life: A Research-Based Experiential Approach, (Belmont, CA: Thomson/Wadsworth, 2007), 127 (quotation in a sidebar box).

47 Richard Conlin, "Chesterton on Humility," The Prodigal Catholic Blog (blog), May 19, 2016, https://richardconlin.wordpress.com/2016/05/19/chesterton-on-humility/.

48 Dan Van Wie, "32 Worst First-Round Draft Picks in NFL History," Bleacher Report, https://bleacherreport.com/articles/980759-32-worst-first-round-picks-in-nfl-history#slide6.

49 Wanderlust Worker, "48 Famous Failures Who Will Inspire You to Achieve," Wanderlustworker.com, https://www.wanderlustworker.com/48-famous-failures-who-will-inspire-you-to-achieve/.

50 Ibid.

51 Claire Cook, Seven Year Switch (New York: Hyperion, 2014).

52 Rich Cimini, "Story of Boy Named Tom Brady," NY Daily News, January 25, 2008, https://www.nydailynews.com/sports/football/giants/story-boy-named-tom-brady-article-1.341686.

53 Chris Chase, "The Best Late-Round NFL Draft Picks Not Named Tom Brady," USA Today Sports, April 25, 2018, https://ftw.usatoday.com/2018/04/2018-nfl-draft-late-round-picks-tom-brady-richard-sherman-kirk-cousins.

Notes (Continued)

54 Mandy Harvey, "Deaf Singer Earns Simon's Golden Buzzer with Original Song," America's Got Talent, June 6, 2017, https://www.youtube.com/watch?v=ZKSWXzAnVe0.

55 Hwai Tah Lee, "Coaching Story: The Battleship on a Collision Course," Coaching Journey, https://coaching-journey.com/coaching-story-the-battleship-on-a-collision-course/.

56 Psalm 119:105.

57 Thomas Rhett, "Life Changes," first released on August 31, 2017, Genius, https://genius.com/Thomas-rhett-life-changes-lyrics.

58 "dynamic," Merriam-Webster.com, https://www.merriam-webster.com/dictionary/dynamic.

59 Goddard Space Flight Center, Risk Management Reporting (Greenbelt, MD: NASA, 2009).

60 Dane Boers, "Beyond the Risk Matrix," ARMS Reliability (blog), September 13, 2017, https://www.thereliabilityblog.com/2017/09/13/beyond-the-risk-matrix/.

61 Ben Bowman, "How Do People Survive Plane Crashes?," Curiosity.com, August 2, 2017, https://curiosity.com/topics/how-do-people-survive-plane-crashes-053cN3Xy.

62 "Smoke Filled Room," Socially Psyched, https://www.dowellwebtools.com/tools/lp/Bo/psyched/16/Smoke-Filled-Room.

63 The Gottman Institute, "Love Lab," https://www.gottman.com/love-lab/.

64 Luke 6:45.

65 "A Quote by Ann Landers," Goodreads.com.

66 Covey, The 7 Habits of Highly Effective People.

67 Wisdom of the Crowd, CBS.com, https://www.cbs.com/shows/wisdom-of-the-crowd/.

68 "Ursula Burns," Forbes, https://www.forbes.com/profile/ursula-burns/#bbdc4db40a0e.

69 Jeannette Nolen, "Ursula Burns" Encyclopedia Britannica, September 16, 2018, https://www.britannica.com/biography/Ursula-Burns.

70 TIME magazine, "Ursula Burns on Distinguishing Herself to Become First Black Woman to Run Fortune 500 Company," YouTube, October 24, 2017, TV interview, https://www.youtube.com/watch?v=r3IcKPQfful.

71 "groupthink, Merriam-Webster.com, https://www.merriam-webster.com/dictionary/groupthink.

72 Tim Fitzsimons, "Meet the Gay Former Liberal Encouraging Others to #Walkaway From Democrats," NBC News, August 21, 2018, https://www.nbcnews.com/feature/nbc-out/meet-brandon-straka-gay-former-liberal-encouraging-others-walkaway-democrats-n902316.

73 Jeremiah 29:11.

74 Proverbs 2:4–6.

About the Author

Amy is the founder of FUSION Leadership Group. After high school, she studied theology at Wheaton College but dropped out after two years to start a family. Twenty years later, she completed her bachelor's degree in Psychology at Liberty University. She also holds a master's degree in Organizational Leadership from South University, as well as several certifications in business, including Project Management Professional (PMP) and Six Sigma. The meshing of the disciplines of psychology, business, and theology shaped her thinking and lead her down the path toward completing *You Can Visit, but You Can't Live There.*

This project is a collaboration of material developed from working in the corporate world, teaching Bible studies, speaking at leadership conferences, and counseling with individuals over a twenty-five-year period. Amy's passion to see young men and women Live Free and avoid the many pitfalls of our post-postmodern culture in America was further forged while helping her young adult children navigate state universities and hold on to their faith and conservative values.

Amy and Perry have been married for thirty years and have three children: Nathan, twenty-six, is active-duty US Air Force; Valerie, twenty-four, is enlisted in the US Air National Guard, works as an assistant project manager for a construction company, and is married to a police officer; Nicholas, sixteen, is a sophomore in high school.

Contact Amy

If you found any of these principles to be helpful, I would love to hear from you. You can email me at:
fusion.group.pgh@gmail.com.

Discounts are available for purchasing this book in bulk. Please contact me at the email above.

FUSION Leadership Group was founded to provide leadership training and resources to under-served populations. Please visit our website for tools and resources. If you would like to hold FUSION Leadership Conferences in your city, please contact us!
www.fusionleadership.site

FUSION Executive Leadership Team

Valerie Donnelly (Amy's daughter)
Amy
Connie Geier (Amy's mom)